T0311746

Cambridge Elements ≡

Elements in Public Policy
edited by
M. Ramesh
National University of Singapore (NUS)
Michael Howlett
Simon Fraser University, British Columbia
Xun WU
Hong Kong University of Science and Technology
Judith Clifton
University of Cantabria
Eduardo Araral
National University of Singapore (NUS)

POLICY FEEDBACK

How Policies Shape Politics

Daniel Béland
McGill University

Andrea Louise Campbell
Massachusetts Institute of Technology

R. Kent Weaver
Georgetown University

CAMBRIDGE
UNIVERSITY PRESS

University Printing House, Cambridge CB2 8BS, United Kingdom

One Liberty Plaza, 20th Floor, New York, NY 10006, USA

477 Williamstown Road, Port Melbourne, VIC 3207, Australia

314–321, 3rd Floor, Plot 3, Splendor Forum, Jasola District Centre,
New Delhi – 110025, India

103 Penang Road, #05–06/07, Visioncrest Commercial, Singapore 238467

Cambridge University Press is part of the University of Cambridge.

It furthers the University's mission by disseminating knowledge in the pursuit of
education, learning, and research at the highest international levels of excellence.

www.cambridge.org
Information on this title: www.cambridge.org/9781108940542
DOI: 10.1017/9781108938914

© Daniel Béland, Andrea Louise Campbell, and R. Kent Weaver 2022

This publication is in copyright. Subject to statutory exception
and to the provisions of relevant collective licensing agreements,
no reproduction of any part may take place without the written
permission of Cambridge University Press.
An online version of this work is published at doi.org/10.1017/9781108938914 under
a Creative Commons Open Access license CC-BY-NC-ND 4.0 which permits re-use,
distribution and reproduction in any medium for non-commercial purposes providing
appropriate credit to the original work is given. You may not distribute derivative
works without permission. To view a copy of this license, visit https://creativecom
mons.org/licenses/by-nc-nd/4.0
All versions of this work may contain content reproduced under license from third
parties. Permission to reproduce this third-party content must be obtained from these
third parties directly.
When citing this work, please include a reference to the DOI 10.1017/9781108938914

First published 2022

A catalogue record for this publication is available from the British Library.

ISBN 978-1-108-94054-2 Paperback
ISSN 2398-4058 (online)
ISSN 2514-3565 (print)

Cambridge University Press has no responsibility for the persistence or accuracy of
URLs for external or third-party internet websites referred to in this publication
and does not guarantee that any content on such websites is, or will remain,
accurate or appropriate.

Policy Feedback

How Policies Shape Politics

Elements in Public Policy

DOI: 10.1017/9781108938914
First published online: May 2022

Daniel Béland
McGill University

Andrea Louise Campbell
Massachusetts Institute of Technology

R. Kent Weaver
Georgetown University

Author for correspondence: Daniel Béland, daniel.beland@mcgill.ca

Abstract: Although the idea that existing policies can have major effects on politics and policy development is hardly new, in the last three decades we have witnessed a major expansion of policy feedback scholarship, which focuses on the mechanisms through which existing policies shape politics and policy development. Starting with a discussion of the origins of the concept of policy feedback, this Element explores early and more recent contributions of the policy feedback literature to clarify the meaning of this concept and its contribution to both political science and policy studies. After exploring the rapidly expanding scholarship on policy feedback and mass politics, this Element also puts forward new research agendas that stress several ways forward, including the need to explain both institutional and policy continuity and change. Finally, the last section discusses the practical implications of policy feedback research through a discussion of its potential impact on policy design.

This Element also has a video abstract: www.cambridge.org
/PublicPolicy_Beland_abstract

This title is also available as Open Access on Cambridge Core

Keywords: policy feedback, mass politics, policy change, policy design, public policy, politics

© Daniel Béland, Andrea Louise Campbell, and R. Kent Weaver 2022

ISBNs: 9781108940542 (PB), 9781108938914 (OC)
ISSNs: 2398-4058 (online), 2514-3565 (print)

Contents

1 Introduction

The claim that existing policies shape the politics of policy development is hardly new and can be traced back to the work of scholars such as E. E. Schattschneider (1935: 288), who, more than eighty-five years ago, famously wrote that "new policies create a new politics." Yet the concept of policy feedback that is widely used today to explore how existing policies shape politics and policy development over time is much more recent (Orloff 1993; Pierson 1993; Skocpol 1992; Weir, Orloff, and Skocpol 1988). What is specific about policy feedback is its temporal emphasis on policy *development* and its claim, in policymaking and politics more generally, that policies are not only effects but potential *causes* (Pierson 1993, 2004a). Over the last three decades, in exploring new empirical and theoretical grounds, the scholarship on policy feedback expanded to focus on the variety of causal mechanisms through which existing policies shape politics and policymaking over time (Béland and Schlager 2019a, 2019b; Campbell 2003, 2012; Jacobs and Weaver 2015; Mettler 2005; Mettler and SoRelle 2018; Patashnik 2008; Patashnik and Zelizer 2013; Weaver 2010).

The main objective of this Element is to review and assess early and more recent contributions to the literature on policy feedback to clarify the meaning of this concept and its contribution to both political science and policy studies. This Element focuses on three related bodies of literature, which cover the most central aspects of the scholarship on policy feedback. Each of the following three main sections features a critical literature review and, in the case of Sections 3 and 4, an agenda for future research on the topics covered.

Section 2 reviews the early literature on policy feedback. As suggested, the concept of policy feedback emerged within historical institutionalism (HI), which has made a strong contribution to both political science and policy studies. Simultaneously, while the section shows that turning to HI is essential to understand the genesis of policy feedback as a concept, it also suggests that other traditions such as punctuated equilibrium (PE) theory and the social construction of target populations have also contributed directly to the field.

Section 3 discusses the evolving literature on policy feedback and the political behaviors and attitudes of mass publics. The section suggests that public policies can influence the behaviors and attitudes of members of the public, with effects on subsequent politics, because (1) they heighten or diminish levels of political participation among those affected, increasing or diminishing political inequality within or between politically relevant groups, and (2) they affect attitudes toward the role of government (sometimes versus the market), support for incumbents and parties, and perceptions of program recipients. These feedback effects vary in their strength and durability.

Section 4 focuses on how policy feedback affects policy change. As suggested, policy feedback mechanisms that affect prospects for policy change are of several distinct types, including economic returns, sociopolitical mechanisms, informational and interpretive mechanisms, fiscal mechanisms, and state capacity mechanisms. Within each of these categories, both self-reinforcing and self-undermining mechanisms exist. Simultaneously, these policy feedback mechanisms can operate in both strong and weak forms, with their impact conditional both on the exact nature of those feedbacks and on how they interact with "exogenous" contextual factors that vary widely across political systems and policy sectors.

The final section turns our attention to the potential contribution of policy feedback research to the world of practice, with a particular focus on policy design. As argued, each of the policy feedback mechanisms outlined in Section 4 can be used by both those seeking to reinforce and those seeking to undermine the status quo to advance their interests. Moreover, efforts to use feedback mechanisms to achieve policy objectives are subject to several constraints, notably the necessity of compromise to achieve policy change and the difficulty of anticipating the effects of some policies. Some strategies, such as "frontloading" policy benefits to secure public support, are likely to be employed by proponents of changes to current policy.

2 Theoretical Perspectives on Policy Feedback

2.1 Historical Institutionalism and the Concept of Policy Feedback

The concept of policy feedback emerged in the 1980s within and at the same time as HI, a broad approach to politics and public policy that is distinct from two other contemporary types of new institutionalism: organizational institutionalism, which focuses on cultural legitimacy and the institutional development of organizations, and rational-choice institutionalism, which focuses on institutional constraints on individual choice (Campbell 2004; Hall and Taylor 1996; on new institutionalism, see Campbell 2004; Lecours 2005; Peters 2011). As the label implies, HI focuses in large part on the evolution and impact of institutional processes over time. It is particularly attentive to the temporal sequence of institutional processes as they unfold over time (Pierson 2004b).

Intellectually, HI is closely related to the idea of *Bringing the State Back In*, the title of a widely cited edited volume published in the mid-1980s (Evans, Rueschemeyer, and Skocpol 1985). Developed in reaction against behavioralist and structuralist approaches that focus on systems theory and class power, respectively, this idea is closely related to the claim that states have a certain level of autonomy vis-à-vis economic and social forces located outside of it (e.g., Campbell 2004; Fioretos, Falleti, and Sheingate 2016; Immergut 1998; Steinmo, Thelen, and Longstreth 1992).

Historical institutionalism emerged in the United States, a country where systems theory and other behavioral approaches to politics had somewhat marginalized the study of the state (Evans, Rueschemeyer, and Skocpol 1985). Yet drawing on existing US scholarship on the state and public policy helped historical institutionalists bring the state back in. The work of Hugh Heclo (1974), who emphasized the role of bureaucrats and policy learning in the development of public policies, proved especially influential. Martha Derthick's (1979) study of Social Security development in the United States drew attention to the role of bureaucrats in defining and expanding the program, a practice closely related to state autonomy. Stephen Skowronek's (1982) book *Building a New American State*, which documented the creation of an administrative state in the United States in the late nineteenth and early twentieth centuries, moved the concept of the state to the center of what became known as American Political Development (APD), a historically minded scholarship on politics and public policy closely related to what would become HI (on APD, see Orren and Skowronek 2004; Vallely, Mettler, and Lieberman 2016).

While born in the United States, HI strongly emphasizes the importance of comparative and international research, stressing how institutions – which are broadly defined as norms and rules that typically include public policies themselves – vary from country to country, which makes comparative research highly relevant. Even some of the early HI studies focusing on the United States have a comparative angle, in part because their objective is to explain what is specific to the United States (e.g., Amenta 1998; Orloff 1993; Skocpol 1992; Weir 1992). Early HI scholarship focused primarily on fiscal and social policy (Immergut 1992; Orloff 1993; Pierson 1994; Pierson and Weaver 1993; Steinmo 1996).

To understand the status of policy feedback within both HI and political analysis more broadly, we can turn to the distinction between the synchronic and the diachronic effects of institutions (Jacobs 2016: 341). First, according to Alan Jacobs (2016: 341),

> A synchronic institutional argument identifies a short-run effect of prevailing political-institutional arrangements on the relative political influence of political actors. Arguments about synchronic institutional effects … take actors' political capacities and policy demands as given and then assess the ways in which the "rules of the game" favor or disadvantage particular types of actors and demands over others.

An early example of synchronic analysis within HI is the work of Ellen Immergut (1992) on "veto points." Studying the politics of health care reform in three European countries, Immergut (1992) suggested that, compared to France and Sweden, the institutional configuration of the Swiss political system, especially federalism and direct democracy, created more institutional opportunities for physicians in Switzerland to successfully oppose health care reforms that they opposed. In general, veto points concern how formal "political institutions shape (but do not determine) political conflict by providing interest groups with varying opportunities to veto policy" (Kay 1999: 406). This is clearly an example of synchronic analysis that stresses how stable "rules of the game" such as federalism and direct democracy shape the constraints and opportunities of political actors involved in the policy process. This type of synchronic analysis about how formal political institutions influence policy behavior has been applied to different policy areas (e.g., Bonoli 2001; Immergut, Anderson, and Schulze 2007; Tsebelis 2002).

In contrast, Jacobs (2016: 344) draws our attention to diachronic factors and processes in political and policy analysis. "Central to diachronic institutional analysis is a fundamentally historical analytical move: the examination of how political structures have, over time, shaped the political capacities and the policy demands that actors bring to the political battlefield" (Jacobs 2016: 344). Just as the concept of "veto points" is an example of synchronic institutional analysis, policy feedback is an example of diachronic institutional analysis (Jacobs 2016: 345). For HI, policy transforms policies into institutions that have much explanatory power in and of themselves. As an exploratory mechanism, therefore, policy feedback is about the *diachronic* (temporal) *political* effects of policies, which are no longer seen only as the effects of politics but also as a potential *cause* of it, *over time* (Pierson 1993).

The claim that existing policies can shape politics and policymaking antedates the advent of the concept of policy feedback, including Heclo's (1974) above-mentioned work on policy learning. Policy learning suggests that existing policies affect the ways in which political actors perceive potential policy alternatives. This discussion about policy learning leads the HI scholar Ann Shola Orloff (1993: 89), when introducing the concept of policy feedback, to quote Heclo (1974: 315): "What is normally considered the dependent variable (policy output) is also an independent variable ... Policy inevitably builds on policy, either in moving forward what has been inherited, or amending it, or repudiating it." This quote not only points once more to the shift from policy as an effect to policy as a cause (Pierson 1993) but also suggests that the institutional effects of existing policies over time can lead to both self-reinforcing and self-undermining processes, depending on the context (Jacobs and Weaver 2015). In other words, the development of these policies is not always about path dependence, which generally refers to how institutions reproduce themselves over time in a specific direction that becomes harder and harder to change as these institutions mature (Pierson 2000). Yet, as we will discuss more systematically in Section 4, most of the scholarship on policy feedback has focused on self-reinforcing rather than self-undermining mechanisms. Thus, the focus has been much more on how policy institutions can foster continuity rather than path-departing change (Jacobs and Weaver 2015). This situation is reflected in the literature review provided in the present section, which focuses primarily on self-reinforcing feedback effects.

Within the HI literature, the term "policy feedback" first appeared in a volume titled *The Politics of Social Policy in the United States* coedited by Margaret Weir, Ann Shola Orloff, and Theda Skocpol (1988). Yet this volume does not explore policy feedback in a systematic manner, something that will only be done a few years later (Orloff 1993; Pierson 1993, 1994; Skocpol 1992). Taking a closer look at some of these seminal publications from the early to mid 1990s is appropriate because it allows us to illustrate three focal points of the early policy feedback literature, which are explicitly discussed and theorized in it: state capacities, interest groups, and lock-in effects (Pierson 1993; Skocpol 1992).

2.1.1 State Capacities

In *Protecting Soldiers and Mothers*, Skocpol (1992: 58) explains how policy feedback can take the form of an expansion of state capacities (on this issue, see also Orloff 1993: 90). This is the case because, as they are being implemented, "policies transform or expand the capacities of the state," while changing "the administrative possibilities for official initiatives in the future, and affect later prospects for policy implementation" (Skocpol 1992: 58). According to Skocpol (1992: 59), a policy can be understood as successful if it leads to an expansion of the "state capacities that can promote its future development, and especially if it stimulates expansion." Here, the idea is that newly established policies can contribute to state-building in a way that, through self-reinforcing processes, promotes future policy expansion.

In *Protecting Soldiers and Mothers*, Skocpol (1992) illustrates this type of policy feedback with the development of the Bureau of Pensions, which was tasked with administering benefits for Union veterans in the aftermath of the US Civil War (1861–5). Because of the gradual expansion of these benefits, Skocpol (1992: 58) suggests, "the Bureau of Pensions became one of the largest and most active agencies of the federal government." The development of Civil War pensions increased state capacities while creating a bureaucratic lobby within the federal government that supported the expansion of the program over time. In the end, however, the relationship between partisan patronage and Civil War pensions weakened support for them and even political momentum for the creation of a broader system of old-age pensions in the United States before the New Deal (Skocpol 1992).

An even more striking case of how policy feedback can increase state capacities and stimulate the formation of bureaucratic lobbies that support the expansion of existing policies is the case of US Social Security, which Derthick (1979) documented long before the concept of policy feedback emerged as an analytical concept. Later scholars have further documented policy feedback related to state-building in the case of Social Security (Béland 2005). Enacted in 1935, Social Security is an earnings-related pension program operated by the federal government. Soon the bureaucrats in charge of the management of Social Security emerged as knowledgeable and skillful allies of the program, which they protected against cutbacks during World War II, when the program faced much political opposition from both within and outside the federal government, at a time when the relatively new program had yet to build a strong constituency of beneficiaries (Cates 1983; Derthick 1979). Later, during the post–World War II era, bureaucrats and political appointees operating within the Social Security Administration (SSA) promoted the expansion of the program by framing the agenda of the regularly held advisory councils tasked to evaluate and make recommendations about the then growing federal social insurance program (Derthick 1979). Over time, SSA officials lobbied Congress and presidents in support of Social Security expansion and the enactment of new social programs such as Medicare, which was adopted in 1965 (Berkowitz 2003; Derthick 1979). Other factors also contributed to the expansion of Social Security and the federal welfare state in the post–World War II era, but the state capacities and internal lobbying power of SSA, itself a by-product of Social Security development, played a major role in the politics of social policy in the United States (Béland 2005; Derthick 1979).

2.1.2 Interest Groups

The second type of policy feedback discussed in *Protecting Soldiers and Mothers* is about how existing public policies can shape the "social identities, goals, and capabilities of groups that subsequently struggle or ally in politics" (Skocpol 1992: 58). This type of policy feedback concerns the impact of existing policies on the development over time of interest groups that have a stake in the policy process (Pierson 1993: 598–605). As Skocpol (1992: 59) puts it, "public social or economic measures may have the effect of stimulating brand-new social identities and political capacities" that may mobilize to preserve existing policies.

In *Protecting Soldiers and Mothers*, Skocpol (1992: 59) shows how the development of Civil War pensions fostered the emergence of interest group organizations organically tied to these public policies. The key organization was the Grand Army of the Republic, the largest organization representing Union veterans. In her analysis, Skocpol (1992: 111) suggests that the expansion of Civil War pensions over time stimulated an increase in the membership of the Grand Army of the Republic, which, in turn, "intensified the interest" of this organization "in pension legislation and administration." This feedback loop led the Grand Army of the Republic to "set up a Washington-based Pensions Committee to lobby Congress and the Pension Bureau" (Skocpol 1992: 111).

More generally, the work of Skocpol (1992) and others (Pierson 1993) suggests that the nature of existing public policies shapes the formation of interest groups and their political mobilization over these policies and within the policy arena. Clearly massive economic and social programs that allocate benefits to large segments of the population are more likely to stimulate the emergence of large and powerful constituencies associated with important interest group organizations that are likely to get involved in the debates over the future of these programs. Conversely, more targeted programs might generate weaker constituencies and related interest groups that have less political clout when the time comes to discuss the future of these programs (Pierson 1994).

These general remarks are illustrated by the HI scholarship on US social policy concerning the contrast between social assistance benefits directed at "dependent" populations and social insurance benefits directed at "advantaged" populations. For instance, Skocpol (1990) wrote about the political weakness of social assistance programs such as Aid to Families with Dependent Children (AFDC), which would end in 1996 as a consequence of the controversial federal "welfare reform" (Weaver 2000). For Skocpol (1990), programs for the poor such as AFDC are "poor programs" that should be replaced by measures offering universal coverage that create broader constituencies and, consequently, more resilient social policies in the long run. Although evidence suggests that some targeted programs such as US Medicaid, which provides health insurance to disadvantaged families and citizens, can grow to generate broader political support over time (Howard 2007), massive social insurance programs that create large constituencies can prove more resilient in the longer term under certain conditions. For instance, this is likely to be the case when these programs generate powerful third-party allies such as governors. The case of the US Medicaid program for low-

income people (Rose 2013) suggests that even programs with weak beneficiaries can become resilient over time if they generate strong political allies.
Large social insurance programs are especially likely to become resilient
when they target politically "advantaged" groups like older people, as is the
case with US Social Security (Campbell 2003; Pierson 1993). The example of
the American Association of Retired Persons (AARP), one of the most
powerful interest groups in the United States, illustrates this reality; this
interest group organization expanded at the same time as Social Security,
before getting involved in the politics of the Social Security reform (on the
AARP, see Lynch 2011). Policy feedback can also shape concrete interest
group organizations over time, a topic studied by Kristin Goss (2012) in her
book *The Paradox of Gender Equality: How American Women's Groups
Gained and Lost Their Public Voice*. In this qualitative analysis of the collective mobilization of women in the United States over more than a century, Goss
(2012: 18) looks at the impact of policy feedback on concrete social move-
ment organizations, an approach that allows her to explore "how different
types of feedback effects interact to affect the scope and nature of groups'
policy engagements." Goss (2012: 184) demonstrates how policies created in
the 1960s shaped the collective action of women in the United States by
offering "tangible antidiscrimination protections that women's groups rallied
to defend and expand" as well as "resources (networks, conferences, money)
to support women's organizing."

2.1.3 Lock-In Effects

Within the HI tradition, the most widely cited publication on policy feedback
is Paul Pierson's (1993) article "When Effect Becomes Cause: Policy
Feedback and Political Change." Although it appeared only a year after
Protecting Soldiers and Mothers (Skocpol 1992), one of the books Pierson
engaged with, this review essay provided a much more systematic take on
policy feedback than anything that had been published on the topic before. In
his article, Pierson (1993) explored issues such as the cognitive side of policy
feedback associated with policy learning and the potential influence of
existing policies on mass politics, thus anticipating what would become
a central avenue for policy feedback research in the years and decades to
come.

Another key contribution of Pierson's seminal article was to introduce the
concept of "lock-in effects" to the policy feedback literature. Drawing on
a recently published book by the economist Douglass North (1990), Pierson
(1993: 608) showed how

Policies may create incentives that encourage the emergence of elaborate social and economic networks, greatly increasing the cost of adopting once-possible alternatives and inhibiting exit from a current policy path. Individuals make important commitments in response to certain types of government action. These commitments, in turn, may vastly increase the disruption caused by new policies, effectively "locking in" previous decisions.

Pierson (1994) applied the concept of policy feedback as lock-in effects in his book *Dismantling the Welfare State? Reagan, Thatcher, and the Politics of Retrenchment.* In this influential book, lock-in effects are especially central to the discussion about pensions reform, with reference to US Social Security. As Pierson (1994: 172) suggests in his analysis of lock-in effects, "sunk costs resulting from previous decisions in pension policy created lock-in effects that greatly constrained Reagan's options on Social Security."

2.1.4 The Multiple Faces of Policy Feedback

Over time, HI generated other perspectives on policy feedback that built on the early scholarship discussed in Sections 2.1–2.1.3 to explore the multifaceted nature of how existing policies can shape the politics of public policy (Béland 2010; Béland and Schlager 2019b). One of these approaches concerns the claim that, just like public policies, state-regulated private social benefits can shape politics over time. Particularly influential here is the work of Jacob Hacker (2002) on how, in the United States, the development of private health and pension benefits has led to the emergence of a "divided welfare state" (the title of his book), in which feedback effects from both public and private social benefits are closely intertwined in both their social functions and the political effects they generate over time. Therefore, it is possible to argue that private benefits "may impact political mobilisation and public expectations in much the same way that widely distributed public benefits do, creating strong political incentives for the maintenance or encouragement of existing private networks of social provision" (Béland and Hacker 2004: 46). The example of health care in the United States perfectly illustrates this claim, as both public policies such as Medicaid and Medicare and private institutions such as health insurance have shaped the politics of reform, including the enactment in 2010 of the Affordable Care Act (ACA) (Jacobs and Weaver 2015). More generally, even when it does not explicitly refer to the concept of policy feedback, the extensive literature on welfare state development demonstrates that the *private* side of policies can shape and constrain *public* policy reform over time (Béland and Gran 2008; Esping-Andersen 1990; Howard 1997; Klein 2003).

Another perspective available in the HI literature is the less developed but promising concept of "ideational policy feedback" (Lynch 2006: 199). This concept refers to how specific ideas and symbols embedded in existing policy institutions can shape the politics of policy reform over time (Béland 2010). For instance, in a book on US social policy, Brian Steensland (2008) argued that the negatively connoted term "welfare" embedded in US social assistance policies contributed to reform failure in this policy area during the 1970s. This was the case because new reform proposals were seen in the mirror of the unpopular and controversial idea of "welfare," which reduced support for them (Steensland 2008). As Steensland (2008: 10) suggests, his case study stresses the role of "*interpretative* feedback mechanisms," which contrast with the "*resource/incentive* dimension of policy feedback processes" associated with lock-in effects (for a recent discussion of ideational policy feedback, see Béland and Schlager 2019b).

For many of the HI scholars cited so far, feedback effects from existing policies appeared as only one type of institutional process among others worth studying to explain policy development. While the expansion of the literature on policy feedback suggests that it now constitutes a stand-alone theory of the policy process (Mettler and SoRelle 2018), returning to the early HI literature has the advantage of reminding us how feedback effects from existing policies do not always tell the whole story about the relationship between institutional processes and policy development. This is something we should keep in mind as we turn to the growing literature on mass politics, policy feedback, and public policy, which is discussed in Section 3.

2.2 Beyond Historical Institutionalism

The discussion so far on HI and policy feedback should not obscure the contribution of other theoretical traditions to the early analysis of how existing policies shape politics and policy development. In this section, we discuss several other approaches that helped shape this analysis.

First, we should mention the work of Theodore Lowi (1964), a US political scientist who explained how specific types of public policy generate distinct forms of politics. His typology is based on the distinction among four types of policy: constituent, distributive, redistributive, and regulatory policies (Lowi 1972: 300). Grounded in the assumption that "policies determine politics" (Lowi 1972: 299), his framework articulates the relationship between these four types of policy with related types of coercion and of politics. In this context, each type of policy is associated with a particular "arena of power" (Lowi 2009) characterized by specific political dynamics. In the United States, this work generated much critical scholarship, including the widely cited work of James Q. Wilson (1973), who revisited Lowi's typology.

In his review essay, Pierson (1993: 625) explicitly mentions both Lowi and Wilson when he rejects what he calls "extremely parsimonious theory linking specific policy 'types' to particular political outcomes." According to Pierson (1993: 625), their typologies are flawed for two reasons: "First, . . . individual policies may have a number of politically relevant characteristics, and these characteristics may have a multiplicity of consequences. Second, . . . policy feedback rarely operates in isolation from features of the broader political environment (e.g., institutional structures, the dynamics of party systems)." From this perspective at least, the emergence of policy feedback as a concept stems in part from a rejection of the abovementioned early policy typologies by Lowi and Wilson (for a critical discussion, see Kellow 2018).

Another stream of scholarship relevant for policy feedback scholarship is the work of the US political scientists Anne Schneider and Helen Ingram on the social construction of target population theory, which stresses the relationship between policy designs and how certain groups are advantaged or disadvantaged in society. Central to the work of Schneider and Ingram (1993) is a typology of target populations based on two criteria: whether these groups are weak or powerful and whether these groups are positively or negatively perceived. This leads to a fourfold typology: advantaged (powerful and positively perceived), dependents (weak but positively perceived), contenders (powerful but negatively perceived), and deviants (weak and negatively perceived). This typology helps scholars understand how policies targeting specific populations are likely to be designed, and how the social constructions embedded in concrete institutional and programmatic designs might shape later policy development through feedback effects.

The final theoretical tradition we turn to in this section, the PE approach, is especially relevant for the development of policy feedback theory, which is why it requires systematic attention. Punctuated equilibrium is associated with the work of Frank Baumgartner and Bryan Jones (see, e.g., Baumgartner and Jones 1993/2009, 2002; Jones and Baumgartner 2005, 2012). Based initially on US experience, the PE approach argues that "Policymaking at equilibrium occurs in more or less independent subsystems, in which policies are determined by specialists located in federal agencies and interested parties and groups. These interests reach policy equilibrium, adjusting among themselves and incrementally changing policy" – a process that they acknowledge "can be profoundly undemocratic" (Baumgartner and Jones 1993/2009: xvii–xviii). Also critical to the PE approach is the flow of information in a policy sector, as well as the limited cognitive capacity and attention spans of policymakers, which tend to filter out information deemed extraneous and policy options that do not fit with dominant policy paradigms favored by actors in the policy subsystems where policy is usually made (Jones and Baumgartner 2005). The result, Baumgartner and Jones argue, is likely to be "periods of stability and incremental drift punctuated by large-scale policy changes" (Baumgartner and Jones 1993/ 2009: xviii) that are "oftentimes disjoint, episodic and not always predictable" (Jones and Baumgartner 2012: 1). These punctuations are frequently initiated when dissident – often newly emergent – groups manage to involve other political actors, widen the scope of political conflict (often by redefining the issue), and shift the political venues where political decisions are made. Policy crises and other "focusing events" often play an important role in these disruptions. Yet these disruptions do not always result in policy change; the interests that benefit from the status quo will use their resources to try to reassert their dominance over policymaking and limit policy changes that harm their interests.

There is much that is shared by the HI and PE perspectives on policy feedback, notably with respect to difficulties in moving away from the status quo that are generated by the unequal distribution of resources as well as shared definitions of policy problems and appropriate responses that are shared by key policy actors. Both incorporate elections and partisan ideological differences, but they are not the primary focus of either the HI or the PE perspective (Jones and Baumgartner 2012: 5–6). There have been important dialogues between the two (see Pierson 2004b), but there are also important differences in the two approaches – some terminological, some merely of emphasis, and others more central to the research endeavor.

One of the most important – and most confusing – differences is in terminology. Historical institutionalists generally refer to elements of current policy that cause it to be stable or expand over time as "positive feedbacks" and those that undermine it, causing it to become less stable or expansive (e.g., lower spending on environmental enforcement or decreased eligibility and lower benefits for public income transfers), as "negative feedback." Writers in the PE tradition, drawing on systems theory approaches, define negative feedback processes as those in which "a disturbance is met with countervailing actions, in a thermostatic-type process" that generally leads to a reversion to the status quo ante, while positive feedback involves disturbances to the status quo in which "change begets change, generating a far more powerful push for change than might have been expected" (Jones and Baumgartner 2012: 3). To reduce terminological confusion, we will largely follow the language of Jacobs and Weaver (2015), drawing on Greif and Laitin (2004), in labeling elements of the policy status quo that tend to hold it in place or lead to its expansion as "self-reinforcing" and those that tend to make current policy more subject to reduction, termination, or transformation as "self-undermining."

Other differences between the two perspectives are more in emphasis. The PE approach gives more attention to the bounded rationality and attention limitations of policy elites. More generally, it gives greater emphasis to the microfoundations of policymaking in information-processing practices, while HI researchers tend to focus more on macro-level forces. Historical institutionalist researchers tend to focus more on relatively slow-moving adaptions of the policy status quo (e.g., the phenomenon of policy drift), while PE researchers give more attention to short-term disruptions, which are often interpreted as exogenous shocks and being subject to fading away rather than processes that are internally generated by the policy itself and likely to be durable (Jacobs and Weaver 2015). But these differences are increasingly of terminology and degree rather than kind. Recent PE scholarship has, for example, devoted increased attention to dysfunctional elements of policies – generally referred to as "error accumulation" (Jones and Baumgartner 2012: 8) – that are not remedied because of resistance from beneficiaries of the status quo, while HI scholarship has moved away from the concept of "lock-in" toward more nuanced views that emphasize both self-reinforcing and self-undermining aspects of policy.

In this Element, we draw on both the HI and the PE perspectives. Although our primary focus is on the HI approach, important insights from the PE approach, including the bounded rationality and limited attention of generalist policymakers, the importance of focusing events, and the potential for exogenous disruptions to existing arrangements, are incorporated elsewhere in this Element, especially in Section 4.

3 Policy Feedback and Mass Politics

Public policies affect not only the interests and capacities of states and interest groups but also behaviors and attitudes among the mass public. A burgeoning literature explores the ways in which policies can increase or decrease political participation among program clienteles and how existing policy can alter attitudes among both the targets of those policies and other members of the public (for earlier reviews, see Béland 2010; Campbell 2012; Larsen 2019; Mettler and SoRelle 2014; Mettler and Soss 2004). Analyses have been growing in scope, with new case studies both within and beyond social welfare policy, where the literature had its starting point. The examination of mass feedbacks in US politics continues, with multiple analyses of the 2010 ACA and new policy areas such as social regulation and rights. To the pioneering work using European data by Svallfors (1997, 2006, 2007, 2010), Kumlin (2004), and Mau (2003, 2004), among others, scholars have added new analyses (Bol et al. 2021; Larsen 2018, 2020; Shore 2019, 2020; Watson 2015; Zhu and Lipsmeyer 2015), while work extends to new locales such as Canada (Gidengil 2020; Soroka and Wlezien 2004, 2010), Africa (Hern 2017; MacLean 2011), Latin America (De La O 2013; Di Tella, Galiani, and Schargrodsky 2012; Manacorda, Miguel, and Vigorito 2011), and Asia (Im and Meng 2016; Li and Wu 2018; Lu 2014; Ricks and Laiprakobsup 2021). Scholars are developing the theory of policy feedback and mass publics with new mechanisms and new contingencies. Methodological sophistication is growing as well with the incorporation of causal models that improve inference.

In this section, we discuss early theoretical perspectives on mass policy feedback, review the major findings on feedback effects in individual-level political behavior and attitudes, examine methodological issues, and suggest new research frontiers.

3.1 Resources, Interpretive Effects, and the Social Construction of Target Populations

Two theoretical perspectives have animated much of the subsequent work on policy feedback and mass politics, suggesting that policies are not just the outcomes of political processes but also important inputs that reshape the political environment by influencing political participation and preferences among members of the public. Paul Pierson (1993) hypothesized that existing policies provide politically relevant resources and convey positive or negative "interpretive" messages to publics about their place in the polity, which affect individuals' attitudes and their propensity to participate in politics. Policies that deliver generous benefits may foster "protective constituencies" that fight against retrenchment, an example of a self-reinforcing effect (Pierson 1994). Working in parallel, Schneider and Ingram (1993) discussed the social construction of target populations, with policies' designs defining clienteles' access to the privileges of social citizenship (e.g., Marshall 1964). Policies for positively constructed groups such as senior citizens tend to be generous and efficiently administered, sending the message that the state perceives these groups as deserving. In contrast, policies for negatively constructed groups such as the poor or criminals are meager and capriciously administered, suggesting that the state considers them marginal members of the polity. In their original formulation, the direction of causality is unclear: Do the policies create the group constructions or do preexisting group constructions lead to differing policy designs (Lieberman 1995)? Recent empirical work has attempted to overcome these challenges with causal models, as we will see in Section 3.4.

Much of the work testing for feedback effects has examined individual-level behavior and attitudes; in Section 4, we examine positive and negative (self-reinforcing or self-undermining) feedbacks at the aggregate level.

3.2 Policy Feedback and Mass Behavior

Feedback studies show that the designs of public policies can increase or decrease the political participation of individuals beyond what we would predict from their education, income, and other demographic correlates of behavior. Many such studies examine the effects of social welfare programs, although recent work has branched out into additional areas such as civil rights, regulations, and criminal justice. Research has sought to uncover the mechanisms by which policies affect behavior and the aspects of program designs that generate these mechanisms. In addition, scholars have explored how policies affect different types of participation as well as participatory level and equality.

3.2.1 Factors in Political Behavior

Political participation is a function of resources, mobilization, and political engagement, factors that arise from preadult socialization and education and from experiences in institutional settings such as work, voluntary organizations, and religious organizations (Verba, Schlozman, and Brady 1995). Policy feedback theory posits that policy experiences affect these drivers of political participation, as well as additional factors that influence political behavior, including stigma, norms, loss aversion, and traceability (Figure 1).

Resources. Policies can confer politically relevant resources such as money, skills, free time, health, and financial stability, which increase participatory capacity and facilitate democratic acts such as voting, contacting elected officials, working on campaigns, attending political meetings, participating in rallies or protests, working with others on political problems, or making political donations. In the United States, Social Security, the federal old-age pension program, enhances the political participation of older US citizens by increasing their free time through retirement and boosting their incomes (Campbell 2003). The 1944 G.I. Bill increased political participation among veterans through enhanced education attainment (Mettler 2005). More recently, Medicaid expansion under the ACA boosted voter turnout among target groups (Clinton and Sances 2018; Haselswerdt 2017), apparently by increasing financial stability and physical and mental health, which are associated with political participation (Ojeda 2015; Pacheco and Fletcher 2015). In Mexico, voter turnout is higher in villages randomly selected for the rollout of a new anti-poverty cash transfer program (De La O 2013).

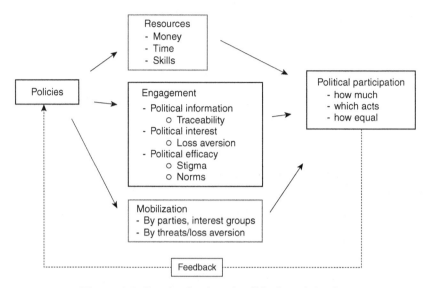

Figure 1 Policy feedback and political participation

Mobilization. Citizens are also more likely to participate in politics when asked to do so (Verba, Schlozman, and Brady 1995). In conferring an age-related social welfare benefit, Social Security in the United States created a politically identifiable group that was subsequently mobilized by interest groups and political parties (Campbell 2003). State laws in the United States that mandate collective bargaining increase the political participation of teachers, apparently through union mobilization (Flavin and Hartney 2015). Under the ACA, social assistance agencies that help customers access health insurance also provide voter registration services, perhaps generating the higher voter participation found in Medicaid expansion states (Clinton and Sances 2018).

Engagement. Political engagement, including political information, political interest, and political efficacy, is another factor driving political participation (Verba, Schlozman, and Brady 1995). Over time, in the United States Social Security increased seniors' interest in politics by tying their well-being to a government program while also enhancing their external political efficacy, the sense that government listens to people like them (Campbell 2003). Recipients of cash welfare who learn how to navigate a complex welfare bureaucracy have heightened levels of internal political efficacy, the sense that they have the competence to negotiate the political realm (Soss 1999). In the United States, veterans who benefited from the G.I. Bill felt "reciprocity," an obligation to participate in civic life in return for the gift of an unexpected education, which may be a form of efficacy as well (Mettler 2005).

Stigmatization and Authority Relations. Not all policy effects are positive. The "interpretive effects" that send messages to program clienteles about their place in the polity (Pierson 1993) have often been used to explain the diminished participation rates of those receiving targeted, means-tested social welfare benefits (Schneider and Ingram's (1993) concept of a negative social construction predicts a similar outcome). Cash welfare in the United States is conferred by gatekeeping case workers whose control over benefits and capricious application of rules undermine the external political efficacy of recipients, reducing their rates of political participation (Soss 1999). Imposing conditionality, such as work requirements, further undermines political participation, as the needed monitoring sends the message that government does not trust the recipient, as the UK case shows (Watson 2015). These negative interpretive effects can be passed on through socialization: Adolescents whose families receive means-tested assistance observe low levels of parental political participation and are less likely to participate in political activities available to youth, such as contacting public officials, boycotting, and discussing political issues (Barnes and Hope 2017).

Targeted programs need not send negative citizenship messages, however. Early childhood programs in the United States and Denmark that incorporate low-income or minority parents into decision-making – allowing such parents to "coproduce" a service they receive from government – enhance parents' skills and knowledge (a resource effect) and send positive interpretive messages that society views them as "capable and valuable" (Hjortskov, Andersen, and Jakobsen 2018), increasing their efficacy and civic participation (see also Barnes 2020; Bruch, Ferree, and Soss 2010; Soss 1999). In the United States, the Earned Income Tax Credit (EITC), which supplements the wages of low-income workers by refunding their income and payroll taxes, generates "feelings of social inclusion" with administration through the universal tax system, not the welfare bureaucracy, and with provision as a lump sum, enabling "patterns of spending and saving that are not possible during other times of the year" and that resemble those of "ordinary" citizens, providing "at least partial access to the social rights of citizenship" (Sykes et al. 2015, 244). Although this study does not examine the political behavior of EITC recipients, feedback theory would hypothesize higher participation rates among EITC recipients than among cash welfare recipients.

Norms. The messages that public policies send may also establish norms that influence political activity. Eileen McDonagh (2010) argues that public policies that "represent maternal traits" send messages about "women's suitability as political leaders"; in nations such as the United States, where maternal traits are demonstrated only in the home, not in the state, McDonagh asserts, fewer women are elected to political office. The provision of new rights may also establish norms enhancing participation. When female student athletes were reminded in an experiment of the purpose of Title IX (to reduce gender-based disparities in US higher education, including athletics), they reported a greater propensity to act to seek equity (although the study did not examine whether such students did act; Druckman, Rothschild, and Sharrow 2018).

Threats and Loss Aversion. Threats to policies may animate political participation as well, given individuals' aversion to losses over equivalent gains (Kahneman and Tversky 1979). In the United States, senior citizens responded to proposed Social Security and Medicare cuts in the 1980s and 1990s with surges in letter-writing to elected officials, the only age group to do so, which helped defeat the proposed reductions (Campbell 2003), an example of the protective constituency dynamic that Pierson posited. Threats emanating *from* policies may also spur participation. In states that expanded Medicaid under the ACA, voter turnout was enhanced not only among Democrats who approved of the law but also among Republicans who opposed it, an apparent "policy backlash" (Haselswerdt 2017). Policies can impose sheer bodily threat that mobilizes as well. The parents of draft-eligible sons in the Vietnam War era were more likely to vote in the 1972 presidential election if their sons drew "losing" draft numbers (although we cannot know from voter records how these parents voted; Davenport 2015). Latinos were more likely to vote in areas where the Secure Communities program rolled out, a program that heightened immigration enforcement by encouraging information sharing between federal and local law enforcement (White 2016). Although government trust fell among Latinos in these areas (see Section 4), the program constituted a threat to families with mixed immigration status and may also have boosted turnout because of mobilization by immigration activists (White 2016). Policies threatening Latinos in California during the 1990s (including Proposition 187, championed by the Republican governor Pete Wilson, which would have banned undocumented immigrants' use of health care, public education, and other services) boosted Latino voters' subsequent turnout and increased identification with the Democratic Party (Bowler, Nicholson, and Segura 2006; Pantoja, Ramirez, and Segura 2001).

Traceability. Whether policies generate feedback effects may depend on their visibility and proximity (Gingrich 2014; Soss and Schram 2007). The Vietnam draft effect in the United States that Davenport (2015) found was concentrated in towns with at least one casualty, increasing the visibility and salience of draft policy. Conversely, when visibility and proximity are muted – for example, when public functions are privatized, obscuring the role of government even when it still funds or regulates the programs – policy effects may not materialize

(Gingrich and Watson 2016). A causal model shows that voter turnout for school board elections in the United States is lower in districts with privately operated charter schools (Cook et al. 2020). The ACA provision allowing people under the age of twenty-six to remain on their parents' health insurance did not increase voter turnout among youth in the United States, despite being popular and widely used; that parental insurance plans are private and funded by the parent may have been more salient than the government's regulatory role in facilitating young people's access (Chattopadhyay 2017).

3.2.2 Behavioral Outcomes

Extant policy feedback studies have examined a variety of behavioral outcomes, including voter turnout, vote choice (see Section 3.3 for effects on incumbent support and favorability), and individual political acts beyond voting, often finding that the provision of benefits enhances participation rates. Scholars have also examined whether program provision can counteract inequalities of participation found in many democracies. Feedback effects on collective forms of political action or nonpolitical acts such as volunteering have been examined as well.

Voter Turnout. The most common behavioral outcome examined in feedback studies is voter turnout, both because of its normative centrality to democratic politics and because of data availability. Policies such as Social Security (Campbell 2003) and the G.I. Bill (Mettler 2005) in the United States as well as experience with public schools and clinics in Africa (MacLean 2011) are associated with greater participation; researchers attribute the participation boost to both resource and positive interpretive effects. Programs in the United States that are means-tested, such as cash welfare, or that are punitive, such as the criminal justice system, are associated with lower turnout (Soss 1999; Weaver and Lerman 2010), apparently because they send negative citizenship messages and because, in the case of the low benefits in US means-tested programs, resource effects are too small to increase turnout. The US Medicaid program is also means-tested, although analyses of its effects on turnout have produced contradictory results. Haselswerdt (2017) and Clinton and Sances (2018) – the latter using a causal model – show that Medicaid expansion during the ACA modestly increased turnout, and the economists Katherine Baicker and Amy Finkelstein (2019) find that the near-randomized expansion of Medicaid carried out by the Oregon Health Insurance experiment of 2008 boosted turnout in that year's presidential election by 7 percent, with particularly strong effects for men (18 percent increase) and in Democratic counties (10 percent increase). But these turnout increases dissipated quickly, and, outside of the ACA, Michener (2018) finds that Medicaid receipt is associated with lower turnout, while the economist Charles Courtemanche and colleagues (2020) find with a causal model that the collective effect of all ACA provisions intended to expand health insurance coverage (Medicaid expansion, the creation of subsidized insurance marketplaces, and various regulations) was only a small and statistically insignificant increase in voter turnout. Claudine Gay (2012) similarly finds that the Moving to Opportunity randomized experiment, which moved low-income people out of high-poverty neighborhoods, reduced voter turnout, with some evidence that disrupted social networks were to blame. Hence, findings on means-tested programs and turnout, both associational and causal, are mixed.

Vote Choice. Policies conferring benefits can result in greater electoral support for incumbent governments. A causal study of state EITCs finds that governors are rewarded electorally for implementing an EITC program, with the largest effects for Republican governors and in counties with many benefiting voters, although the effects dissipate over time (Rendleman and Yoder 2021). The implementation of an EITC in Italy similarly benefited incumbents electorally (Vannutelli 2019). A causal analysis shows that a Romanian government program giving poor families coupons for computer purchase increased support for the incumbent governing coalition (Pop-Eleches and Pop-Eleches 2012), while the De La O (2013) causal study of the Progresa conditional cash transfer program in Mexico found both greater turnout and greater support for incumbents in villages with longer exposure to the program.

Political Activity beyond Voting. Some studies examine policy feedback effects for other political acts. The development of Social Security over time increased US seniors' rates of contacting elected officials and of donating to and working on political campaigns (Campbell 2003). Program receipt can heighten rates of "civic participation," such as working with others in organized groups (e.g., Mettler 2005). Farmers receiving payments from the US Department of Agriculture are more likely than other agricultural producers to run for office (Simonovits et al. 2021).

Equalizing Effects. In many democracies, political behavior is stratified by income and education. Redistributive public policies can offset this effect by enhancing resources and other politically relevant factors for the less privileged. Because in the United States Social Security constitutes a higher share of poorer seniors' incomes, they are more likely to vote, contact elected officials, and make campaign contributions with the program in mind than are higher-income seniors, making seniors' overall political participation less unequal than it would otherwise be (Campbell 2003). In that country, the educational benefits of the G.I. Bill had a curvilinear effect, boosting the civic participation of veterans from middle-income backgrounds more than those from lower-income families (for whom the resource boost was insufficient to spur great participation) or higher-income families (who would have enjoyed higher educational attainment anyway; Mettler 2005). The participatory effects that MacLean (2011) found in Africa are also offsetting: The most impoverished people in rural areas are the most likely to use public services and in turn are the most likely to participate in politics. Across European countries where greater early childhood expenditures and cash benefits increase voting among single mothers, the largest effects are for middle- and higher-income lone mothers, so these programs equalize participation between lone mothers and other demographic groups but not among such mothers (Shore 2020).

Behavioral Feedbacks beyond Individual-Level Political Participation. Finally, policies can affect nonpolitical participation. Across the Organisation for Economic Co-operation and Development (OECD), government social welfare retrenchment is associated with more volunteering, a behavioral feedback outside of politics (Suzuki 2020). And policies can affect group behavior, for example in locales where government programs are inadequate. In Zambia, low levels of government service provision encourage higher levels of collective behavior in which communities organize to respond to the need left by the "gap the state left," as opposed to individual-level feedback (Hern 2017).

3.3 Policy Feedback and Mass Attitudes

A second stream of research examines how existing policies affect *attitudes* among the public, both those policies' target populations and other members of the public. The policy feedback literature argues that the designs of policies affect the drivers of attitudes, and as with studies of political behavior, research has sought to determine the mechanisms by which this effect materializes. The outcomes examined include attitudes toward programs themselves or their recipients and how policies affect attitudes toward government and toward the market.

3.3.1 Factors in Attitudes

Individuals' attitudes toward political objects arise from preadult socialization; symbolic attachments including partisanship, ideology, and racial sentiment; group attachments; self-interest and material stakes; personal experiences; and elite framing and priming. The policy feedback literature argues that the designs and effects of public policies can also affect attitudes, either because they alter some of these factors, such as self-interest and personal experience, or because

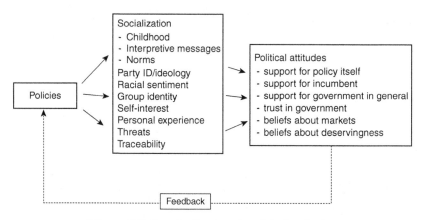

Figure 2 Policy feedback and political attitudes

they alter the conditions that allow these factors to function, such as making more or less visible the material stakes in government activity (Figure 2).

Self-Interest and Personal Experience. The resources that many public policies confer constitute a material stake that may enhance individuals' support for a given program. Survey respondents using subsidies or gaining insurance through the Affordable Care Act are more likely to say that the law has had a favorable impact on health access (Jacobs and Mettler 2018); similarly, approval of the ACA is higher in Medicaid expansion states, with the largest increase among lower education nonsenior adults, the expansion's target population (Sances and Clinton 2021). Universal policies are typically more popular than targeted ones (Cook and Barrett 1992), perhaps because more people see themselves as current or potential beneficiaries. A US-based survey experiment finds that support for tuition-free college falls when the benefit is targeted to low-income families relative to a universal program design (Bell 2020).

Personal policy experience may also counteract the influence of other predispositions such as party identification. In the United States, those receiving Medicare (those just over the age sixty-five eligibility threshold, compared to those just under) are more supportive of Medicare spending and the ACA, with the effect stronger among Republicans (Lerman and McCabe 2017). Similarly, the gap between Republicans and Democrats in ACA favorability is smaller among those who gained insurance through an ACA marketplace compared to those with employer-based insurance (McCabe 2016).

Threats. The asymmetry of gains and losses (Kahneman and Tversky 1979) means that threats to policies, both proposed and realized, affect attitudes just as they do behaviors. In the United States, ACA approval was higher in Medicaid expansion states compared to non-expansion states but only after the 2016 election made Republicans' repeal threats more credible (Sances and Clinton 2021). When reduced benefits and stricter requirements for a universal Danish educational grant were announced while the European Social Survey was in the field, those interviewed after the announcement expressed less satisfaction with government compared to those interviewed earlier, particularly among those more likely to be affected by the cuts (Larsen 2018).

Proximity, Visibility, and Traceability. This last result suggests that proximity, visibility, and traceability affect the likelihood that public policies will shape attitudes. In cases where policy changes have not produced attitudinal changes, lack of proximity or visibility is usually suspected. For example, the 1996 welfare reform in the United States, which imposed time limits and work requirements on cash assistance precisely in line with public objections to the program, did not make citizens more supportive of program spending, warmer toward program recipients, or more supportive of the party that forged the reform, the Democrats (Soss and Schram 2007). Lack of proximity may explain the reform's failure to induce attitudinal change: Many people do not participate in cash welfare or know someone who does.

Privatized policies may also hide the government's role, shaping attitudinal feedbacks. Across European countries, there is less support for government spending on health care where health care is more privatized (Zhu and Lipsmeyer 2015). At the same time, in countries where health care is privately financed and where individuals must weigh different public or private alternatives, their personal experience matters more for their attitudes toward government; but where health care is entirely public and universal, personal experiences are divorced from perceptions of the role of government (Larsen 2020).

"Interpretive" or Citizenship Messages. Paul Pierson (1993) argued that policies could influence mass behaviors and attitudes not only through the resources they confer but also with the "interpretive" messages they send. Many analysts have pointed to such messages – which tell individuals how important or worthy they are in the view of the state – as the apparent mechanism linking policy designs with attitudinal outcomes, even though the data necessary to test for such mechanisms is rarely available in extant studies.

In the United States, welfare case workers' arbitrary and capricious powers over benefits send messages to the recipients that they are unworthy, diminishing their political efficacy and leading them to view the entire government as arbitrary (Soss 1999), while recipients of the universal Social Security program have higher efficacy than other citizens (Campbell 2003). Similarly, Swedish citizens in universal programs that treat clients as empowered "customers" express greater trust in politicians, more support for increased social spending, more leftward ideological placements, and greater interpersonal trust than those experiencing income-targeted "client" programs (Kumlin 2004; Kumlin and Rothstein 2005). In the UK, making receipt of cash assistance conditional on working, and then monitoring recipients' compliance, sends the even harsher message that government does not trust recipients (Watson 2015).

Policies beyond the social welfare arena send interpretive messages too. An analysis combining survey data with the size and racial composition of jail inmate populations at the county level in the United States finds that, where criminal justice enforcement is more racially skewed, highly educated Black respondents are less likely to say government is responsive, have less trust in government, and become less participatory. At the same time, white respondents in areas with large Black populations and racially skewed enforcement exhibit higher trust, political interest, and nonelectoral participation. Criminal justice disparities apparently signal to Blacks that government is targeting them while signaling to whites that government is "looking out for them" (Maltby 2017: 544).

Elite Framing and Priming; Media and Party Effects. The ways in which political elites such as elected politicians and bureaucrats talk about programs and clienteles – and the considerations they prime in citizens' minds – may affect attitudes as well. European analysts argue that existing policy regimes serve as channels of socialization and elite framing, with extant policies defining the national "moral economy," a macro-level interpretive feedback that affects what publics support (Lindh 2015; see also Mau 2003, 2004; Svallfors 1997, 2006, 2007, 2010). In the United States, studies show that citizens have certain racialized policy images in their heads, with universal programs like Social Security coded as "white" and cash welfare and many other means-tested programs coded as "Black," in part because of elite framings (Winter 2006) and media portrayals (Gilens 1999) that overrepresent those racial groups. The media may also increase the visibility of policies, increasing awareness and policy effects on attitudes above and beyond any resource effects, as studies of education reform in China (Lu 2014) and water privatization in Argentina (Di Tella, Galiani, and Schargrodsky 2012) show.

The effects of policies on attitudes may also depend on the messenger. Lindh (2015) finds that class differences in support for market models of welfare distribution are greater where there is more public delivery (in Nordic countries) and smaller where there is more private delivery (in Anglo-Saxon countries and Japan). The difference seems driven by the presence of unions and parties in the Nordic states, whose rhetoric emphasizes class-based politics, while such collective organizations and therefore class-based rhetoric are more muted in the other contexts.

3.3.2 Attitudinal Outcomes

Policy feedback scholars have examined a variety of attitudinal outcomes ranging from policy effects on attitudes toward programs and their recipients, toward the incumbent government that delivered the policy, or toward government in general (or toward market-based provision). Some of these effects are self-reinforcing, strengthening political support for subsequent rounds of policymaking, while some are self-undermining, undercutting support and leading to negative policy spirals. The discussion in Section 3.3.1 of factors in attitudes mentioned some attitudinal outcomes along the way; here, we cite additional studies on outcomes.

Program Support; Reinforcing and Thermostatic Effects. Policies may generate their own support, with attitudes toward programs becoming more favorable among those who benefit, as several studies of the Affordable Care Act have shown (Hopkins and Parish 2019). Individuals receiving benefits from the relatively new Chinese welfare state become more likely to see the government rather than individuals as responsible for citizen well-being (Im and Meng 2016). Conversely, government spending can elicit a "thermostatic" effect, with the public responding to increased spending with preferences for cutting spending or responding to a reduction in spending with preferences for more government activity, as studies of the United States, United Kingdom, and Canada demonstrate (Erikson, MacKuen, and Stimson 2002; Soroka and Wlezien 2004, 2010; Stimson 2004; Wlezien 1995). Thermostatic effects are stronger on issues of high salience and in unitary (rather than federal) systems and stronger for some issues in presidential rather than parliamentary systems (Soroka and Wlezien 2010).

Attitudes toward Program Recipients. Policies may also alter views about societal groups that ordinarily arise from preadult socialization or group orientations, with policies and their designs sending messages to other members of the public about the perceived worth and deservingness of public policy clienteles (Schneider and Ingram 1993). In the United States, Bell's (2020) survey experiment finds that support for tuition-free college is higher when a minimum high school grade point average is included as a requirement, apparently boosting the perceived deservingness of recipients. Also, in that country, Social Security Disability Insurance recipients, even though they are recipients of a contributory, earned social insurance program, are deemed as less deserving by experimental subjects when they are portrayed in vignettes as suffering from "harder-to-diagnose impairments" such as mood disorders (Fang and Huber 2020).

Attitudes toward Incumbent Governments. Public policies may affect attitudes toward the government that produced the policy in question, as when satisfaction with the incumbent Danish government fell after education grant cuts were announced in the middle of the European Social Survey (Larsen 2018). Conversely, support for government can rise with a policy intervention: Using survey data collected immediately before and after COVID-19 lockdowns were implemented in European countries in spring 2020, Bol and colleagues (2021) find that lockdowns increased satisfaction with democracy and vote intentions for the party of the incumbent prime minister or president. A causal study of a temporary anti-poverty cash transfer program in Uruguay found higher government support among recipients than among a control group, with the effect persisting after the program ended (Manacorda et al. 2011).

Trust in Government. The COVID-19 lockdowns that Bol and colleagues (2021) examined also increased trust in government. Across European countries, trust in government is greater where welfare spending is higher (Shore 2019). Li and Wu's (2018) causal model shows that the rollout of a new rural pension scheme in China increased trust in both local and central government. In the reverse direction, negative policy experiences can undermine trust, as Maltby's (2017) study of racial disparities in US criminal justice enforcement showed for Black respondents.

Issue Ownership. Related to incumbent support, policy feedbacks might affect "issue ownership," citizens' perceptions about which political parties are best at handling which issues (Petrocik 1996). A study examining forty-six issues across seventeen rich democracies (including many European countries, the United States, Canada, Australia, and New Zealand) found that issue ownership is quite stable, with right-of-center parties having ownership over public finance, law and order, immigration, and international affairs issues and left-of-center parties having ownership over the welfare state and the environment (Seeberg 2017). One question is whether the implementation of new policies can shake up these patterns. An examination of a major Medicare reform in the United States suggests that the answer is no: Although majorities of panel survey respondents knew that Republicans had designed the popular new prescription drug benefit and had controlled government at the time of passage, that knowledge did not make them more likely to say that Republicans would do a better job managing entitlements or conducting health policy in the future (Morgan and Campbell 2011). Issue ownership resembles attitudes toward program recipients in its stickiness: The images in people's heads about political parties and about program recipients have proven largely impervious to policy feedbacks. Partisan shifts in vote share or party identification due to policy are typically ephemeral (Galvin and Thurston 2018).

Beliefs about Markets. With many rich democracies introducing privatized elements into public policy, attitudes not just about government but about the role of markets could be affected. Cross-sectional analysis of support for the market distribution of social services shows greater support in advanced democracies with more private spending, suggesting "the operation of normative feedback effects flowing from existing welfare policy arrangements" (Lindh 2015; see also Di Tella, Galiani, and Schargrodsky 2012). The proposed mechanism is the message sent by existing policy: "A market-based social service system might nourish beliefs that social services are 'normal' commodities suitable for market distribution, while a system of public provision might encourage the conception that services constitute social rights that are to be provided independent of market logic" (Lindh 2015: 893). Cross-sectional, regime-wide analyses cannot combat the alternative hypothesis that some countries have more private spending because public opinion was more supportive of market-oriented policy to begin with. But an analysis of surveys conducted before and after the 2003 market-model Medicare reform in the United States found that senior citizens getting prescription drugs from private insurance companies became no more likely to support the reform or other market-model reforms like Social Security privatization than seniors with only traditional, government-only Medicare (Morgan and Campbell 2011).

Norms. Other policy changes have been found to create new norms. Longitudinal studies show that individuals became more supportive of smoking bans after their adoption in France, Germany, and the Netherlands (Mons et al. 2012) and became more likely to view secondhand smoke as harmful and to view smokers with disdain in the United States (Pacheco 2013). In the United States, after the Iowa Supreme Court upheld same-sex marriage, apparently sending messages from elites about what is socially acceptable, support for same-sex marriage increased (Kreitzer, Hamilton, and Tolbert 2014). The increase in the availability of public childcare in Norway increased mothers' likelihood of saying public childcare is best (Ellingsaeter, Kitterod, and Lyngstad 2017).

3.4 Data and Models

Considerable advances have been made in the data and models utilized in policy feedback work. Earlier models relying on cross-sectional data faced the challenge that reported differences in attitudes and behaviors between two programs could simply be due to preexisting differences in the two programs' clienteles, not the effects of the programs themselves. Inference has improved with the use of longitudinal and panel data, which, over time, examine individuals whose policy experiences are changing, increasing certainty that any observed attitudinal or behavioral changes can be attributed to policy; beyond the examples cited in Sections 3.2 and 3.3, Jacobs and Mettler (2018) examine attitudes and behaviors as some panel respondents gained health insurance during ACA implementation. Other studies have capitalized on graduated treatments, where the outcomes of interest vary with the magnitude of policy experience. Bruch, Ferree, and Soss (2010) show that, in the United States, client efficacy varies across means-tested programs of varying levels of paternalism; Weaver and Lerman (2010) show that, in the same country, more severe encounters with the criminal justice system have greater negative effects on subsequent political participation.

The greatest improvements in inference have come from the use of causal models. The ideal way to determine whether effect X causes outcome Y is to randomly assign some subjects to the treatment while retaining others as a control; random assignment ensures that the groups do not differ in systematic ways so that any difference in the outcome can be confidently attributed to the treatment. Sometimes social scientists can randomly assign treatments, as when conducting survey or field experiments. A field experiment assigning some consumers seeking health insurance under the ACA to the US government's healthcare.gov website while directing others to a private interface, health-sherpa.com, found that Republicans are more likely to sign up for insurance with the private interface (Lerman, Sadin, and Trachtman 2017). Survey experiments in that country have also found greater support for tax expenditures than for direct spending programs aimed at the same goal (Ashok and Huber 2020; Faricy and Ellis 2014).

Often, however, random assignment is not available to social scientists for ethical or practical reasons. An alternative approach is to capitalize on natural or quasi-experiments, in which groups are exposed to experimental and control conditions by factors outside the investigator's control in ways that resemble random assignment. Examples include Davenport's (2015) use of the US Vietnam draft lottery in explaining parents' subsequent electoral turnout and Larsen's (2018) use of a cut to a Danish education credit announced in the middle of survey data collection to assess satisfaction in government. A similar approach exploits the staggered rollout of programs, using longitudinal data and difference-in-differences (diff-in-diff) models to compare changes in outcomes over time between a group subject to a new policy and a group that was not, which serves as the control. Examples include Li and Wu's (2018) study of the new rural pension scheme in China, implemented in waves over a three-year period; Pacheco's (2013) study of state-level smoking bans, whose varied timing enabled a causal estimate of their attitudinal effects; and White's (2016) study of the Secure Communities policy, whose staggered implementation facilitated a causal estimate of the program's effect on Latino turnout in affected counties. Several scholars have used diff-in-diff models on Medicaid expansion and non-expansion states to measure the attitudinal or behavioral effects of the ACA (Clinton and Sances 2018; Haselswerdt 2017; Sances and Clinton 2021). Regression discontinuity design (RDD) models compare groups lying closely on either side of a cutoff (in geo-RDD models, the threshold is physical, such as a state border), under the assumption that they are similar (or not different in ways that are correlated with the intervention) even though they are not randomly assigned. Lerman and McCabe (2017) used regression discontinuity to compare the attitudes of those immediately above and below the age of Medicare eligibility. A similar approach examining the attitudes of residents of apartment buildings above and below the threshold for public versus private garbage collection finds differences arising from policy: Those who think they have private garbage service rank it as superior to public service, even when they in fact have public service (Lerman 2019).

Although the use of survey and field experiments, natural experiments, and RDD and geo-RDD designs has put the policy feedback field on much firmer inferential footing, such causal models raise important theoretical questions. If the designs of public policies affect attitudes and political behavior among members of the public, over what time frame do they do so and by what mechanism? Some scholars examine whether attitudes vary across different national welfare regimes and find that those living in regimes with more privatized programs are more supportive of market-model programs (e.g., Gangl and Ziefle 2015; Lindh 2015). Here, the mechanism seems to be socialization: Those growing up with privatized provision, or who experience it for many years, are more accepting. As Gangl and Ziefle (2015: 513) put it: "welfare states [reflect] but also [shape] the moral economy of modern societies, where citizens' belief systems are inherently affected by those norms that are institutionalized in and legitimized by public policy environments." The downside is that we cannot know from these typically cross-sectional, observational studies whether the extant form of social provision caused these attitudes or whether countries whose populations were already more supportive of private provision designed their welfare systems concomitantly. Hence the move to causal models. But causal models make their own troublesome assumptions: that policy change acts like a "flipped switch" and that policy feedback can occur in the short term. Sometimes we observe such short-term effects arising from policy change (Ellingsaeter et al. 2017) and, sometimes, we do not (Morgan and Campbell 2011; Soss and Schram 2007). As Julianna Pacheco (2013) notes, it can take time for a new norm to be established.

3.5 Lingering Questions and New Directions

The literature on policy feedback and mass publics has made considerable strides, both theoretically and empirically. The methodological advances are particularly exciting, with causal models providing greater confidence that the behavior and attitudinal effects detected are actually due to policies and not merely to selection effects or preexisting differences.

Questions remain, however. While some work cites political parties, interest groups, and the media as mechanisms linking policies with attitudes and behaviors, more research is needed. In addition, most individuals have multiple policy relationships with government, some of which may be cross-cutting: A given individual might receive Social Security in the United States, a universal program with positive attitudinal and participatory effects, as well as food stamps, a means-tested programs with negative attitudinal and participatory effects. Scholars have just begun to explore the net effect of multiple experiences (e.g., Rosenthal 2019). "New" social risks such as the increase in lone motherhood, challenges to family formation, and the growth of low-wage and gig economy "outsider" jobs that lack protections and benefits deserve examination for the ways in which existing policies fail to keep up, leaving gaps that may generate feedback effects. New country cases are always welcome as well. One lingering question is the generalizability of findings from the United States and Europe, where feedback research has been concentrated. And there is much to be in done in exploring the ways in which institutional arrangements – and other conditions – heighten or obscure feedback effects (but see Soroka and Wlezien 2010). Work on federalism in the United States, for example, has begun to explore these interactions (e.g., Michener 2018).

Feedback scholars must also do more to incorporate the role of race and ethnicity. Jamila Michener (2019) argues that, particularly in the United States, race affects the operation of policies (because of unequal treatment across racial groups) and therefore the mass and elite feedbacks that emerge. Chloe Thurston (2018: 163) shows that the long history of civil rights organizations and social movements has been a struggle about visibility, an effort by the marginalized to expose the "uses of state power against racial minorities as a way of contesting it." Scholars must consider how the operation of feedbacks may be different for the marginalized in many societies. More feedbacks research is needed on the interaction between (often biased) institutional arrangements and individual-level characteristics; nowhere is this more pertinent than with such vulnerable groups.

Finally, the literature needs to expand the list of outcomes examined. Many behavioral studies only examine voter turnout because of data availability, but there are many other types of behavior to examine if we had the data. Jamila Michener's (2018) use of "fair hearings" in Medicaid cases suggests the use of administrative data may open additional avenues of inquiry.

4 Policy Feedback and Policy Change

This section focuses on how policy feedback affects *subsequent policy change* or the *absence of policy change*. Policy change is broadly conceived here to include changes in formal policies (policy choices), changes in the policy that is delivered or not delivered (policy outputs), and the impacts of that policy and their relationship to policy goals (policy outcomes). The discussion here largely excludes effects on policy goals – the degree to which objectives were achieved – and the experience of program "clients" (see, e.g., Herd and Moynihan 2019) except insofar as they ultimately feed back into later rounds of policymaking or incremental adjustments in policy. The section will draw upon rich literatures that examine policy feedback in both the HI and the PE traditions; it will also draw on other literatures such as policy learning to incorporate a broader range of policy feedbacks that cross sectoral and geographic boundaries.

We begin by distinguishing between feedback *causal mechanisms* and feedback *effects*, a distinction that is often obscured in the literature. We then discuss how the literature has categorized feedback effects on subsequent policymaking and policies. Effects on *politics*, which were addressed in detail in the previous section, will be considered in less detail and primarily as they relate to future rounds of policymaking rather than to first-order effects on public mobilization and public opinion. While policy feedback effects may be broadly categorized as self-reinforcing or self-undermining, we also discuss additional dimensions of feedback effects – for example, their strength, intentionality, and timing.

We then discuss the many different types of policy feedback *causal mechanisms* and the conditions that contribute to those mechanisms being felt in stronger or more muted forms. Finally, we briefly address how policy feedback mechanisms are likely to operate differently in democratic and authoritarian societies and suggestions for future research.

4.1 Causal Models of Policy Feedback Effects

The literature on policy feedback effects on policy stasis and change has been characterized by substantial confusion over causal mechanisms and effects. The intuition underlying the concept of policy feedback is a simple one, as shown in Figure 3: Policy X at a particular point in time (t_1) influences Policy X at a later time (t_2) through a feedback causal mechanism. Turning that simple intuition

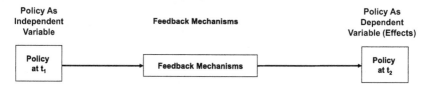

Figure 3 A simple model of policy feedback mechanisms and policy effects

into a set of testable propositions and assessing evidence about their impact is decidedly more complex, however; it is a multistep process, with intricacies at each step, as shown in Figure 4. First, which aspects of Policy X at time t_1 are the cause? Is it the official policy *choice*, usually imbedded in a law of regulation, or is it the policy *outputs* delivered or left undelivered, or the policy *outcomes* – what actually resulted from the policy as delivered? All three have been used as causes in analyses of policy feedback effects on policy change.

Second, research on policy feedback effects is generally distinguished from studies of policy implementation – that is, how policy choices are turned into policy outputs and outcomes, the process shown on the left-hand side of Figure 4. Like policy implementation, there is usually a time lag between the adoption of a policy choice at t_1 and the policy outputs and outcomes at t_2. Yet policy feedback involve processes of *mediation and transformation* as well, shown in the middle part of Figure 4, through processes of public opinion change and civic engagement discussed in the previous section, as well as other feedback mechanisms to be discussed in Section 4.3 on causal mechanisms.

Third, studies of policy feedback often seek to define the exact *causal mechanism* through which policy at time t_1 affects later policy developments. Social scientists are increasingly concerned with not just ascertaining the correlational relationship between independent and dependent variables but also understanding *how* that relationship is created. Is it by facilitating enduring political coalitions that support or oppose the policy? By creating or reducing fiscal room for a policy or its expansion? By reducing attention paid to an issue by busy policymakers or cognition of potential alternatives? Or is it some combination of two or more of these mechanisms? The middle section of Figure 4 outlines a series of potential policy feedback mechanisms. These will be given detailed discussion in Section 4.3.

Fourth, most studies of policy feedback and policy change are interested in assessing the *feedback effect* – that is, the impact of the causal mechanism on policy at t_2. As will be discussed in the next section, feedback effects have multiple dimensions, and different studies have focused on different

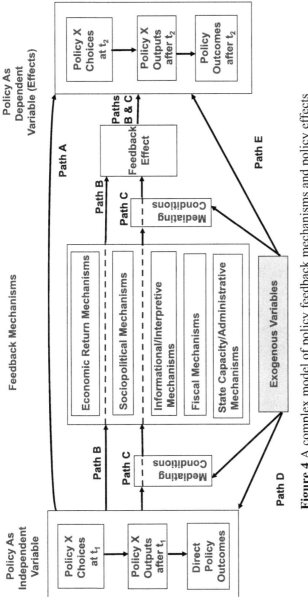

Figure 4 A complex model of policy feedback mechanisms and policy effects

dimensions. Moreover, the feedback effect usually cannot be observed directly; it must instead be inferred from observing the policy at t_2 and comparing it to that at t_1, as shown on the right-hand side of Figure 4. And the same complexities that hold on the independent variable side hold for the visible explanandum: Is what is being explained the policy choice or the output or the outcome at time t_2? Different studies focus on different aspects of policy at t_2.

A final complexity concerns the role of exogenous variables, which can include everything from patterns of interest group power to the ideology of the governing party and the structure of the political institutions. As shown at the bottom of Figure 4, exogenous variables can influence developments at each stage of the causal chain – and this has important implications for assessments of the impact of policy feedback mechanisms. Most notably, they can have direct effects on policy at both t_1 and t_2, as shown in Paths D and E; these are usually not considered feedback effects. It may be difficult to separate out whether policy at t_2 is the result of feedback effects (Paths B or C) or the direct effect of the exogenous variables. For example, if a politically powerful trucking industry and auto users lobby in Country X manages to create an earmarked motor fuel tax dedicated to highway spending, while a weaker industry in Country Y does not, that creates a potential fiscal feedback mechanism. But if Country X later spends more, and more consistently, on highways than Country Y, is that necessarily the result of the existence of the earmarked revenue source (Path B) or the combination of an earmarked revenue source mediated by elite acceptance in Country X of the idea of earmarking to ensure a credible and steady commitment of funds for this purpose, as well as continuous fiscal austerity pressures in Country Y that were stronger than those in Country X (Path C)? Or is it simply the result of continued power differentials between the two constituencies (Paths D and E) (see Dunn 1978). The different causal paths can be very difficult to disentangle.

Exogenous variables can also have a critical impact on the causal mechanisms themselves. The goal of most analyses of policy feedback mechanisms is to ascertain the impact of those mechanisms on policy at t_2, that is, to assess the *endogenous* sources of policy stasis and change (Path B). Yet a pure separation from exogenous factors is almost impossible in the real world – policy feedback mechanisms are likely to be shaped by the interaction of endogenous impacts of the policy and exogenous factors (Path C); looking only at feedback mechanisms that are entirely untainted by external factors is likely to lead to a small and unrepresentative universe of cases. We will address these interactions in more detail as we look at individual policy feedback mechanisms in Section 4.3.

4.2 Dimensions of Feedback Effects

The literature on policy feedback effects has addressed at least six dimensions of those effects – direction, strength, timing and duration, scope, traceability, and intentionality – often without distinguishing carefully between them (for a discussion, see Busemeyer, Abrassart, and Nezi 2021). These dimensions are summarized in Table 1.

Direction of Policy Effects. As noted in Section 2.3, the different connotations of "positive" and "negative" feedbacks used by authors in the PE and HI traditions have resulted in substantial terminological confusion. Hence in what follows we will utilize the less confusing labels of "self-reinforcing" and "self-undermining" (Jacobs and Weaver 2015). But even this terminology suggests dualistic categories of "self-undermining" and "self-reinforcing" that are too simplistic, as several authors have pointed out (see, e.g., Busemeyer et al. 2021). Self-reinforcing policy feedback effects most obviously concern causing a policy to be sustained at something very close to its current level and

Table 1 Spectrums of variation in policy feedback effects

Dimension	Subdimension	Range and Variation
Directionality	Self-Reinforcing	Stabilizing – Adapting – Expansionary/Intensified
	Self-Undermining	Layering – Contractionary – Terminating or Regime Transitioning
	Mixed	Self-Reinforcing Dominant – Offsetting – Self-Undermining Dominant
Strength		Strong – Muted – Absent
Timing and Duration	Stability	Consistent – Punctuated
	Duration	Fleeting – Temporary – Long Term – Permanent
	Onset	Sudden Shock – Slow-Moving
Scope		Program or Policy-Specific – Sector-Specific – Spillover – General
Traceability		Visible – Invisible
Intentionality		Intended – Partially Intended – Unintended – Unanticipated – Unwanted

form of operations. But stability is not the same thing as rigidity; the term has also been used to describe outcomes including adaptation to shifting conditions with relatively modest adjustments. Indeed, a program that is overly rigid may be less likely to be sustainable in achieving program objectives in the long term (Patashnik and Weaver 2021). Moreover, program *expansion* (e.g., increasing benefits or coverage in income transfer programs or increased subsidies for wind and solar power development) has also been included within the rubric of self-reinforcing direction – it clearly should be seen as a continuum rather than a simple effect.

While these self-reinforcing policy feedback effects were the primary initial focus of the HI approach, more recent research suggests that the "capacity of public policies to remake politics is contingent, conditional, and contested" (Patashnik and Zelizer 2013: 1072). It even raises the contrasting possibility that policies may be "self-undermining," that is, that policies will give rise to forces that will lead to those policies being cut back, terminated, or radically transformed. In the discussion of feedback mechanisms in Section 4.3, we will see that many of the mechanisms that give rise to self-reinforcement may under some conditions be self-undermining instead. Yet even where major policy change does occur as a result of self-undermining policy feedback, it will not be written on a blank slate. In his discussion of pension policy "regime transitions" – that is, fundamental shifts in the organization, justifications, and distribution of costs and benefits – in wealthy democracies, for example, Weaver (2010) argues that which regime transition options are open to governments are heavily constrained by the fiscal, political, and redistributive impacts of the policy regime already in place.

Policy feedback effects – from both individual mechanisms and multiple mechanisms – need not be unidirectionally self-reinforcing or self-undermining. They can also be complex, and mixed, in their impacts (Moore and Jordan 2020; Skogstad 2020). This is particularly true of policies that have multiple intertwined components. Hobbs and Hopkins (2021), for example, find that the effects of different components of the ACA on support for the Act roughly offset each other in the aggregate, with different components affecting different groups in opposite directions.

The balance of policy feedback effects may also change over time. In her study of European biofuels policy, Grace Skogstad (2017) found that, in the early years of the program, those impacts were largely self-reinforcing, as the policy built support from a broad coalition of farmers, biofuels manufacturers, and environmental groups. However, as the negative effects of biofuels on land use and food prices were better understood, some elements of the coalition turned to opposition, and the balance of policy feedback effects moved from one in which self-reinforcing effects were dominant to one in which self-undermining effects became stronger, but with both effects still being present; the result was a cutback in EU policies that supported biofuel production but not their complete abolition. Similarly, fossil fuel interests and electric utilities in the United States increased their mobilization against state clean energy policies once they realized that "these laws could add significant costs to their bottom lines and threaten their existing assets" (Stokes 2020: 6).

Strength of Feedback Effects. While directionality has been the focus of research on policy feedback effects, it has not been the only one. Research suggests that feedback effects vary substantially in their strength. Some policies do not become deeply entrenched, for example because the constituencies that they create or strengthen are still relatively small, under-resourced, or stigmatized. The continued under-resourcing could arise from the policy itself, if the benefits being provided are too small to meaningfully boost resources of the program constituency. Weak policy feedbacks may also result from conscious efforts by program opponents – for example, efforts by Republicans to delegitimize the Affordable Care Act of 2010 (Patashnik and Zelizer 2013; Jacobs and Weaver 2015).

Timing and Duration of Policy Effects. The effects of policy may vary on several dimensions, notably their *stability, duration, and onset*. Regarding stability and duration, the early work by Pierson (1994) in the HI perspective focused on relatively slow-moving processes that produce policy effects that are quite stable over time, such as support of seniors in the United States for continued levels of Medicare spending. Studies in the PE tradition have focused on more short-term processes and effects that are more short term and reversible, such as increases in media attention and issue salience, elite attention, and public support for changes in the status quo after mass shootings and other focusing events. But, as suggested in the case of EU biofuels policy, policy effects may shift over time, and even fleeting or temporary policy feedback effects may be important if they prompt a government response that is enacted at a peak in the "issue attention cycle" and is durable once attention fades.

Feedback effects may also vary in their *onset*. As noted earlier in this section, one of the major differences between PE and HI approaches to policy feedback is the types of feedback effects they tend to emphasize. For PE theorists, sudden shocks that create focusing events are critical in getting policymakers to pay attention to an issue. Historical institutionalists, on the other hand, tend to focus on more slow-moving processes such as the development of constituencies around social programs.

Scope. Feedback effects can also vary in the scope of their effects (Busemeyer et al. 2021) – both in the policies involved in creating the feedback and in the policies affected by it. Some feedback effects are relatively narrow, originating in and affecting only a particular program or even part of a program. Frequently, however, feedback effects are felt more broadly on programs in the same policy sector or even as "spillover effects" into neighboring – and sometimes seemingly unrelated – policy sectors. For example, Cruz Nichols and colleagues (2018) found that, in communities subject to intensified immigration policing, there was lower trust of government as a source of health information among both native and immigrant US Latinos, which could potentially affect their enrollment in health care programs under the Affordable Care Act. Vesla Weaver (2007: 230) and others have argued that victories in the 1960s by proponents of civil rights for African Americans in the United States resulted in what she calls:

> *frontlash* – the process by which formerly defeated groups may become dominant issue entrepreneurs in light of the development of a new issue campaign . . . The same actors who had fought vociferously against civil rights legislation, defeated, shifted the "locus of attack" by injecting crime onto the agenda. Fusing crime to anxiety about ghetto revolts, racial disorder – initially defined as a problem of minority disenfranchisement – was redefined as a crime problem, which helped shift debate from social reform to punishment.

And some policy effects originate in and are felt more generally across a broad range of sectors. Suzanne Mettler (2011), for example, argues that the heavy reliance of the US government on invisible "submerged state" policies makes them less visible to their recipients and empowers powerful interests and intermediaries, weakening the potential for bolder government policy actions in the future. Another example of "broad origin–broad impact" policy feedback is the potential for rapid expenditure growth in a set of policy programs to "crowd out" expenditure growth in – or even the creation of – other programs in a period of fiscal austerity.

Traceability/Visibility. As Pierson (1993: 622; see also Arnold 1990) has noted, traceability "involves two distinct tests: can visible outcomes be linked to government policy and can those policies be linked to someone who can be given credit or blame?" Politicians may attempt to manipulate traceability for both political and policy ends. In 2020, President Trump insisted that his name go on COVID relief checks, a break from normal Treasury Department practice, to try to maximize personal political credit for the payments (Olorunnipa and Rein 2020; Rein 2020). Intentional manipulation of traceability can also be used to try to limit blame for unpopular actions – for example, legislation increasing the age of eligibility for public pensions often includes long delays between the enactment and when it goes into effect. Such changes are likely to both lower attention paid to the initiative in the short term and weaken opposition from groups most likely to object (those who are close to retirement age) because they have no time to adjust their behavior. This in turn makes it less likely that there will be strong political pressure to repeal the policy change and more likely that people will adjust their retirement age expectations and behavior by the time the policy becomes effective. But Suzanne Mettler (2011, 2018, 2019) argues that policies that have low visibility and traceability – like the tax expenditures that she argues play a substantial role in the "Submerged State" in the United States – are also less likely to reap political support for an activist government and for the political parties that support such a role for government.

Intentionality. Policy effects also vary in the degree to which they were intended by those who created the policy. Of course, most policymakers, having invested time and political capital in developing a policy, do not want to see it be dismantled or even eroded over time. They may even hope for an expansionary dynamic: that, once created, one or more of the policy mechanisms discussed in Section 4.3 will cause the program to generate demands for or at least facilitate program expansion. Maltzman and Shipan (2012: 114) argue that legislators in the United States seek "both to lock in policy gains and to secure programs that automatically will be revised in ways consistent with his or her preferences." There are some historical episodes that are consistent with this view. The US Social Security program, for example, was seen by President Franklin Roosevelt as a program that would be impossible to dismantle because contributors would feel that they had earned their benefits; and some of its architects, notably Wilbur Cohen, clearly saw it as a vehicle that would allow incremental expansions or "slices" that eventually would make "a nice sandwich." More recently, the Policy Feedbacks Project in the United States has sought to develop principles to incorporate answers to the question "Will this policy create positive political effects – that is, will it encourage ongoing and, ideally, increasing efforts to address the problem?" (Hacker and Pierson 2019: 9) into the crafting of policy proposals and their strategic management. When this high degree of intentionality and planning is involved, we can think of feedback effects as "Designed."

In practice, policymakers often do not think strategically about feedback effects on later policy changes at t_2 – especially those effects that occur mostly in the long term. In countries such as the United States, where policy initiatives are subject to revision or even being blocked altogether during the legislative process, or in coalitional and minority government parliamentary systems, where support for a package acceptable to all partners must be negotiated, short-term deal-making considerations rather than long-term feedback effects are likely to be the primary consideration. With the 2010 Affordable Care Act, for example, Oberlander and Weaver (2015) have noted that broadly popular provisions such as forbidding coverage to persons because of preexisting conditions were "front-loaded" (went into effect almost immediately), while unpopular provisions such as a charge for individuals who did not secure insurance were "back-loaded" (went into effect later). Overall, however, Eileen Burgin (2018: 299) argues that the congressional architects of the ACA "neither carefully considered the impact of Congress's pre-enactment choices on the ACA's future trajectory, nor anticipated implementation and sustainability challenges." She attributes this lack of attention to several factors, including the primacy of making sure that some legislation was enacted, overwork, and the very limited room for negotiation and adjustment at the end stages of the congressional enactment process, given its unusual legislative trajectory. In cases of lower levels of intentionality and strategizing about feedback mechanisms – which are almost certainly more common ones than "Designed" processes – feedback effects can be considered "Intended" or even "Partially Intended." In political systems such as in the United States, where many policy decisions are the result of complex compromises, "Partially Intended by Some" is probably a more accurate description of intentionality.

At the other end of the intentionality spectrum, policy effects may be "unintended" or even "unanticipated" (de Zwart 2015); the former suggests that policy designers foresaw negative effects as possible but accepted the risk as being worth it for potential gains, while the latter suggests that they did not see it all. Leah Stokes (2020: chap. 2) has outlined several factors, including complexity of legislation, uncertainty around the effects of innovative policies, time constraints during the legislative process, and complexity of jurisdiction, that may lead to policy consequences different than those involved in enacting a policy may have anticipated. Policies may of course also be "unwanted" but enacted over the objections of some interests who accepted them either as the cost of getting other things they did want or because they lacked the power to block the change. They may also be *both* unforeseen and unwanted, though these categories are separate. Unintended and unwanted consequences are likely to have self-undermining effects by reducing confidence in the policy, the government that imposed it, or both. The phenomenon that Jacob Hacker (2004, 2019; see also Galvin and Hacker 2020) has labeled *policy drift* generally involves policy outcomes that are both unanticipated and unwanted; these outcomes "result not from 'formal revision', but from policies' failure to adapt to shifts in their social or economic context" (Béland, Rocco, and Waddan 2016: 201–202). For example, nonmandatory, tax-advantaged employer-sponsored pension programs that long provided an important source of income to retirees in the United States and Canada became less able to do so as broad economic shifts led to a drop in coverage in those plans and led an increasing number of employers to shift their plans from a defined benefit to a defined contribution basis, shifting risk from employers to employees (Hacker 2019: chap. 5). Additional exogenous factors that make policy drift more likely include strong political opponents of changes in policy choices (formal policy provisions) and outputs as well as numerous and strong veto points in the political system that create high hurdles to program revisions (Hacker, Pierson, and Thelen 2015: 180).

4.3 Feedback Mechanisms

What causes the multidimensional feedback effects outlined in Section 4.2 and explains whether these effects are self-reinforcing or self-undermining? Under what conditions are specific feedback effects more or less likely to occur? In this section, we will analyze five broad types of policy feedback mechanisms – economic returns, sociopolitical, informational/interpretive, fiscal, and state capacity/administrative – although the boundaries to these categories are not rigid and there is significant overlap between some of them. These mechanisms incorporate the resource and interpretive factors that were the focus of Paul Pierson's (1993, 1994) early work on policy feedback as well as later iterations (Hacker and Pierson 2019) and work by scholars in the PE tradition and other streams of research. As shown in Table 2, these causal mechanisms focus on different sets of actors, ranging from political and administrative elites to the mass public, as well as different reasons for engagement by those actors.

Before beginning, several caveats are in order. First, while causal mechanisms are sometimes analyzed in a dichotomy between endogenous (generated by the policy itself at t_1) and exogenous (generated by external forces) mechanisms, very few phenomena can be cleanly differentiated as "purely" endogenous or exogenous. In the real world, elements of both are almost always intertwined. Most feedback mechanisms involve interaction between policy-induced developments and environmental (exogenous) factors that mediate and shape their impact. Climate change, for example, is not purely exogenous because it derives in large part from governmental policies that have encouraged exploitation of fossil fuels and kept their prices low, especially in countries where domestic energy production was seen as a source of energy security. And the power of a constituency that was created or strengthened by policies at t_1 to consolidate and strengthen its policy gains (endogenous mechanism) will be magnified when a political party that is sympathetic to their objectives holds office or has important leverage over parties that do hold power (exogenous mechanism). Thus, German wind power advocates were aided in their efforts to secure and

Table 2 Self-reinforcing and self-undermining feedback mechanisms and effects

Mechanism Type with Main Causal Mechanism	Key Actors	Direction	Key Strengthening (+) and Weakening (−) Parameters of Policy Affecting Mechanism	Facilitating (+) & Limiting (−) Exogenous Conditions for Operation of Mechanism
ECONOMIC RETURNS				
Increasing Returns: Path dependence results from high setup, learning and coordination costs, and anticipated reactions, **or**	Variety of social, economic, and political actors	Self-Reinforcing	+ High transition costs of plausible policy alternatives increase resistance to change + High policy "maturity"	+ Strong multiple veto points in policymaking process − Enactment during economic downturn may weaken investments in policy by potential supporters
Diminishing or Static Returns: Path departure resulting from minimal or decreasing returns		Self-Undermining	+ Low transition costs of plausible policy alternatives reduce resistance to nonincremental change	+ Weak veto points in policymaking process
SOCIOPOLITICAL				
Concentrated Constituency Benefits and Resources:	Program beneficiaries	Self-Reinforcing	+ Flow of program benefits are concentrated, traceable	

Flow of concentrated benefits to constituency reinforces sense of entitlement and strengthens organizations capable of defending benefit stream if threatened, **or**

to program, and begin quickly after program is initiated

+ Program gaps provide opportunities for client group organization

– "Half solutions": Groups that receive some benefits from policies have reduced incentives to organize for expanded or improved program

+ Multiple veto points increase strategic leverage of status quo defenders

– Beneficiaries of status quo ante at t_1 policy are unorganized and receive diffuse benefits

– Program is enacted just before shift in institutional control to hostile political party

– Fiscal stress weakens opportunities for program expansion

Concentrated Constituency Losses: Perception of concentrated losses by some constituencies leads to development or strengthening of coalitions seeking policy change and/

Constituencies harmed by policies

Self-Undermining

+ Policy produces substantial costs for powerful constituencies

+ Concentrated policy costs emerge quickly after enactment of policy reform

+ Concentrated and organized constituency is strongly united in support of benefits under status quo ante

+ Constituency political leverage increases with

Table 2 (cont.)

Mechanism Type with Main Causal Mechanism	Key Actors	Direction	Key Strengthening (+) and Weakening (−) Parameters of Policy Affecting Mechanism	Facilitating (+) & Limiting (−) Exogenous Conditions for Operation of Mechanism
or to fragmentation of existing support coalitions			+ Costs were unanticipated by constituency groups, especially in innovative programs	+ change in party control of government + Program can be challenged in several venues + Implementing agencies or governments are hostile to program
Mass Public and Party Support: Perception of widespread benefits increases perceptions of satisfaction in mass public, or	Mass public, plus party elites and media, who frame and prime public perceptions	Self-Reinforcing	+ High salience of program benefits	+ Political leaders claim credit for program benefits − Low level of partisan polarization among electorate and party elites
Mass Public and Party Opposition: Perception of widespread losses increases		Self-Undermining	+ High issue salience of program failures	+ High-profile opinion leaders have electoral incentives to frame program as loss-

perceptions of grievance in mass public

imposing or flawed or con-stituency as undeserving
+ Negative focusing event increases issue salience and undermines confidence in program
- Issue attention cycle lessens general public attention over time
- Repeated failure of reform efforts discourages further investment in reform initiatives
- High partisan or ideological polarization
- Low trust in government

+ Freedom of media and social media

INFORMATIONAL/INTERPRETIVE

Information: Policymakers consider program revisions based on information about its effects

Politicians, based on input from media, citizens, interest

Varies depending on information available to

Table 2 (cont.)

Mechanism Type with Main Causal Mechanism	Key Actors	Direction	Key Strengthening (+) and Weakening (−) Parameters of Policy Affecting Mechanism	Facilitating (+) & Limiting (−) Exogenous Conditions for Operation of Mechanism
	groups, policy evaluators	policymakers and framing		
Elite Attention Overload: Limited elite attention and processing capacity and low issue attention outside core constituencies lowers incentives and ability of elites to address nonurgent issues, **or**	Core constituency groups and policymaking elites, plus outside groups mobilized by policy focusing events	Self-Reinforcing	+ Low issue salience for public outside core constituency + "Half solutions" weaken urgency for elites to address issue	− Exogenous policy shocks disrupt policy equilibrium and mobilize usually inattentive groups/elites + High insulation of policy-making institutions into effective "policy monopolies"
Punctuated Attention: Focusing events compel elites to respond		Self-Undermining	+ High issue salience for general public + High credit-claiming opportunities for politicians for intervention	+ Strong external shock compels elite attention and mobilizes outside interests + Weak insulation of sectoral policymaking + Alternative decision venues available

Positive Social Construction: Program clientele viewed as deserving of program benefits promotes program stability or enhancement	Program clientele, public and administrators	Self-Reinforcing	+ Program financed by beneficiary contributions
Negative Social Construction: Program clientele viewed as undeserving of program benefits promotes program retrenchment or abolition		Self-Undermining	+ Program identified with socially stigmatized groups
Menu Contraction: Constituency and elite satisfaction with program narrows agenda to	Political elites and policy sector experts	Self-Reinforcing	+ High transition costs of plausible policy alternatives

Table 2 (cont.)

Mechanism Type with Main Causal Mechanism	Key Actors	Direction	Key Strengthening (+) and Weakening (−) Parameters of Policy Affecting Mechanism	Facilitating (+) & Limiting (−) Exogenous Conditions for Operation of Mechanism
incremental program fixes, **or**				− Beneficiaries of current policy are unorganized and receive diffuse benefits
Menu Expansion: Constituency and elite dissatisfaction with program leads to search for nonincremental program fixes		Self-Undermining	− Concentrated policy costs emerge quickly after enactment of policy reform + Incremental policy "patches" have been implemented but fail to address perceived policy problems − Viable plausible models for policy regime transition exist or can be created	− Concentrated and organized constituency was strongly united in support of benefits under status quo ante and have a strong ethical sense of entitlement + Multiple sources of policy expertise exist
FISCAL **Earmarked Financing:** Dedicated revenue stream provides adequate funding for foreseeable future,	Program agency leaders and budget guardians	Usually Self-Reinforcing	− Large and rapidly growing program expenditures raise strong concerns among budget guardians	− Difficult overall fiscal climate

leading to limited attention and concern by budget guardians			
Trust Fund Crisis and Automatic Stabilizing Mechanisms: Insufficient dedicated funding to meet program commitments sparks intervention or automatic cuts	Usually Self-Undermining of Policy Choice Stability and Policy Outcomes		+ Prohibitions or limitations on general revenue funding for program + Demographic or cost trends undermine adequacy of dedicated financing mechanism or declines in revenue source
Crowding Out: Increased programmatic or general fiscal stress strengthens pressures to reduce program spending or forego expansion and new program initiatives	Self-Undermining	Program agency leaders and budget guardians	+ Rapid and unanticipated program growth + High levels of overall fiscal stress inhibit expansion of existing programs and creation of new ones

STATE CAPACITY AND ADMINISTRATIVE ARRANGEMENTS

Self-Reinforcing Supply-Side Feedbacks: Policy providers use political	Self-Reinforcing	• Program providers within	+ Program providers are well-organized, politically + Electoral and legislative systems give policy

Table 2 (cont.)

Mechanism Type with Main Causal Mechanism	Key Actors	Direction	Key Strengthening (+) and Weakening (−) Parameters of Policy Affecting Mechanism	Facilitating (+) & Limiting (−) Exogenous Conditions for Operation of Mechanism
influence to pursue program expansion	government or private or NGO sectors		resourceful, and united in support of program + Program is close to core missions of agency	providers strong political leverage
Self-Undermining Supply-Side Feedbacks: Policy providers use political influence to resist program expansion and/or promote retrenchment or policy drift		Self-Undermining	+ Program is subject to turf battles	+ Electoral and legislative systems give policy providers strong political leverage
Means/Ends Match: Administrative agency has resources, mission, and mandate that allow it to achieve policy goals, *or*	• Administrative agency leaders and program operators	Self-Reinforcing	+ Relatively simple tasks consistent with implementing agency skills and resources	+ Simple administrative arrangements requiring minimal cooperation of actors with conflicting goals

	Self-Undermining
Means/Ends Mismatch: Administrative mismatch leads to failures that damage administering agency's and program's external reputation and political support	+ Complex and intrinsically difficult tasks inconsistent with organizational missions + Inadequate resources to achieve agency mission + Administrative responsibilities are divided among multiple entities with conflicting organizational mandates and priorities

Source. This table draws on Oberlander and Weaver (2015), Weaver (2015), Patashnik and Zelizer (2013), Patashnik (2019), and Patashnik and Weaver (2021).

maintain favorable policies to aid the development of wind power by the growth of the Greens in the Germany at the federal and *land* levels, while US wind power advocates suffered important policy reversals when the Republicans came into power (see, e.g., Karapin 2014; Stokes 2020). For each mechanism, we will discuss mediating conditions that influence various dimensions of those mechanisms' feedback effects (i.e., their direction, strength, temporality, etc.); the best statements will usually involve the caveat "under these conditions."

Second, these causal mechanisms are not mutually exclusive. On the contrary, they are likely to operate simultaneously, though not necessarily in the same direction. Arguments that increasing returns to public policies tend to prevent a major deviation from those policies present a persuasive case about barriers to transformational policy change, for example, but they become more compelling if they are combined with sociopolitical mechanisms that show how those mechanisms motivate important political and economic constituencies or mass public opinion.

Finally, most of the causal mechanisms discussed here can be either self-reinforcing or self-undermining, depending on the parameters of the mechanism and/or the impact of exogenous mediating conditions. In Table 2, policy feedback mechanisms that are derived from the same causal dynamic but differ in their direction based on the impact of specific parameters or exogenous influences are discussed together. Equally important, "policies may generate self-reinforcing and self-undermining feedback effects simultaneously; ... the balance of these feedback effects may shift over time; ... [and] it is the balance of these effects that matters politically" (Oberlander and Weaver 2015: 58) in determining overall feedback effects.

4.3.1 Increasing Returns

One of the most cited policy feedback mechanisms draws on Paul Pierson's argument about increasing returns. Based on arguments in institutional economics developed by Brian Arthur (1989) and others, increasing returns to choices made early in the policy development process ("critical junctures") mean that "the *relative* benefits of the current activity compared with other possible options increase over time [and] the costs of exit – of switching to some previously plausible alternative – rise" (Pierson 2000a: 252). This happens through one or more barriers to policy change:

(1) *large setup costs* that would require major new investments to change (e.g., shifting from driving on the right-hand side of the road to the left);

(2) *learning effects* as people and businesses get higher returns from gaining skill in operating in accordance with a new policy;

(3) *coordination effects* as returns increase from operating in a consistent manner (e.g., all motor vehicles driving on the same side of the road). As Pierson notes, this is consistent with the notion of "institutional complementarities" developed by Hall and Soskice (2001) to explain continuing differences between – and stability within – models of liberal and coordinated market economies;

(4) *adaptive expectations* as individuals change their behavior to respond to revised policy even if they were originally opposed to it and continue to suffer losses from it, because they need to make investments to operate consistently with current policy (Pierson 2000a: 254).

An important implication of this argument is that policies become more difficult to reverse the more "mature" they are – that is, the longer they have been in place and affected constituencies have adapted their expectations and investments to those policies. More generally, while Pierson uses the term "lock-in" to describe these processes of path dependence, especially in his earlier work, this does not mean that he viewed programmatic choices as immutable but rather as costly to reverse; the logic of increasing returns is that, even when institutional barriers to policy reversal are minimal, the collective gains from policy stability make policy reversals (and repeated policy gyrations as governing parties with different ideologies and policy priorities move into and out of office) relatively rare.

While the increasing returns causal mechanism relates primarily to the economic calculations of various societal actors, political factors also play an important role. Pierson (2000b) argues that the short time horizons of politicians make them less concerned about the long-term efficacy of policies. In addition, political institutions that may impose multiple veto points and supermajority requirements for policy change inhibit later policy shifts. Recognizing the importance of policy stability for encouraging investment around an initially controversial policy or institutional choice, governments may even develop mechanisms to demonstrate a "credible commitment" that a policy will not be reversed.

The centrality of increasing returns arguments in the policy feedback literature on policy change raises important questions about their limitations, however. Are all public policies subject to increasing returns or do some policies provide static or diminishing returns over time? Urban highway construction that simply results in more traffic, more pollution, and neighborhood disruption as well as mass incarceration as a means of crime control (Dagan and Teles 2014, 2016) are among the policy sectors where research suggests that diminishing returns – not just to achieving policy objectives but also to building political constituencies – may occur. Moreover, transitioning away from some policies may have relatively low economic costs, especially when doing so involves eliminating a policy that has visible costs and does not require heavy investment in new physical or administrative infrastructure – elimination of the one-child policy in China, for example. In addition, whether policies are enacted during good or bad economic times may affect their durability: Enactment during economic downturn may weaken investments in a policy by potential supporters and thus lower the transition costs of abandoning it (Karch and Rose 2019: 26–27).

4.3.2 Social-Political Mechanisms

A variety of social-political policy feedback mechanisms are discussed in the literature, and these mechanisms are often discussed in conjunction with ideational and other mechanisms as jointly causing feedback effects. In the discussion here, we will focus on mechanisms that assert an important role for the power of concentrated constituencies – and especially power asymmetries between constituencies – as well as mass political beliefs and political institutions.

Constituency Resources and Power. One of the most powerful mechanisms favoring self-reinforcing policy effects concerns the role of organized constituencies: Established policies are likely to foster the growth of supportive constituencies, especially by groups that are "rent-seekers" – those that are trying to extract resources for themselves from the rest of society. Indeed, the "constituency power" feedback mechanism is building on the increasing returns mechanism by focusing on the *distributive* consequences of increasing returns. Constituency groups are frequently better organized to protect their interests than the public, especially when that policy provides *concentrated benefits* to key constituencies of the policy. Equally important, policies may channel *political, economic, and ideational resources* to those groups that they can use in later conflicts over the policy. In countries that have adopted import substitution industrialization policies, for example, both industries and workers employed by those industries are likely to derive benefits from tariffs and from other restrictions on imports. In many policy sectors, such as pensions, people feel that they have earned a *right* to the benefits that they receive, especially if they have contributed to them through payroll taxes. The flow of concentrated benefits to a constituency over time reinforces a sense of entitlement and strengthens organizations capable of defending that benefit stream when it is threatened. Pierson (1994) argued that, in wealthy democracies, these constituency effects have supplanted support from labor unions and political parties on the left as the dominant protectors of welfare state programs from cutbacks when fiscal constraints are strong. Self-reinforcing constituency policy feedback may also lead to program expansion when there are no politically powerful opposing interests and fiscal constraints are relatively weak.

The power of constituency groups to produce self-reinforcing feedbacks is also influenced by that program's *political opportunity structure*: "specific configurations of resources, institutional arrangements and historical precedents for social mobilization" (Kitschelt 1986: 58) of specific latent or already organized constituencies. These opportunity structures may affect both a constituency's ability to influence the formulation of policy choices and the implementation of those choices. In some cases, opportunity structure is partially endogenous to the policy, since specialized structures may be established as part of the policy that grant some constituencies privileged access both to the policy and to its implementation, while excluding other constituencies.

The discussion in this section makes clear that the power of constituency groups to take advantage of and build on self-reinforcing policy feedback is conditional rather than absolute. Several scholars, writing about the United States, argue that specific programmatic features may either strengthen or weaken the constituency benefits and resources feedback mechanism. On the one hand, several scholars have noted that gaps in coverage in the Medicare program for the elderly offered an opportunity for AARP, the largest advocacy organization for the elderly in the United States, to attract members by offering insurance policies to address those gaps. On the other hand, Andrea Campbell (2011) has discussed what she calls the demobilizing effects of "half solutions": If a policy adopted offers a partial solution to a problem, the very existence of "a" solution, even if not an optimal solution, may undermine broad constituency mobilization for a better or a more comprehensive solution. The US health care sector offers many examples of this phenomenon. Creation of the Medicare and Medicaid programs in the United States, for example, addressed – albeit very incompletely – coverage for two of the groups that are hardest to serve through market solutions, the elderly and the poor. This undermined the potential for mobilization for a program with universal or quasi-universal coverage (Campbell 2011; Hacker 1998; Morgan and Campbell 2011).

In recent years, research has pointed to several conditions under which alignments of constituency power may produce limiting and even self-undermining feedback effects as well as self-reinforcing ones. Patashnik and Zelizer (2013) have noted that coalitions that support a policy change may disintegrate after their favored policy is enacted and supporters stop investing in it. Policies may also turn out to have more beneficial elements for some parts of the initial support coalition than for others, causing the latter to withdraw or waiver in their support. As a result, long-term policy resilience depends on "whether a reform sustains the coalitions that brought it about or *causes* new coalitions to emerge *after* enactment" (Patashnik and Zelizer 2013: 1074; see also Karch and Rose 2017). Aseema Sinha (2019: 58) sees just such a process as critical to the heavily contested economic reforms in India after 1991, arguing that, while the reforms encountered opposition from business, farmer, and labor interests, and substantial reversals, "what sustained this shift was the disruption of old coalitions, and the creation of new supporters and their role in consolidating the reform program despite opposition."

Several factors can strengthen or weaken self-reinforcing constituency resources and benefits. Several authors (see, e.g., Berry, Burden, and Howell 2010; Campbell 2012; Karch and Rose 2017) have noted that *timing* matters: Programs enacted just before a shift in party control of government not only may fail to gain from increasing returns but also may fail to benefit from a growing sense among the constituency of entitlement to benefits and (potentially) a flow of resources over time.

Other conditions may lead to more clearly self-undermining policy effects. A perception of *concentrated losses* by some constituencies is likely to lead to the development or strengthening of constituencies seeking policy change and/or to the fragmentation of existing support coalitions. Jacobs and Weaver (2015) argue that a constituency-based mechanism for self-undermining feedbacks could develop even for powerful interests if the constituency accepted a policy at t_1 that offered short-term benefits but imposed long-term costs, or if unanticipated losses result from compromises made during the process of policy adoption. The layering and interaction of multiple policies over time that were difficult to predict in advance could also lead to self-undermining constituency feedbacks. Leah Stokes (2020: 5), in discussing the reversal of several US state initiatives to promote clean energy under pressure from fossil fuel interests, similarly notes that the nature and severity of "policies' potential outcomes are hard to predict, particularly with innovative laws that have not been trialed extensively in other jurisdictions." Highly complex, multicomponent legislation also contributes to what Stokes calls "the fog of enactment." As those new policies are implemented, "actors learn, they update their beliefs and come to attack policies they previously ignored or underestimated" (Stokes 2020: 4). They may invest more resources in political action and, in the United States and other systems of multilevel governance, build networks that cross jurisdictional boundaries to improve their information, update preferences, and learn what strategies are effective in recouping past policy losses (Stokes 2020: chap. 2; see also Hertel-Fernandez 2019).

Several other endogenous and exogenous factors are also likely to contribute to self-undermining effects that may lead to policy change. If concentrated policy costs emerge quickly after enactment of policy reform, for example, constituency groups that perceive themselves as losers will have invested less in adaptation and will be more likely to resist. Moreover, constituency political leverage may be uneven over time and increase with a change in party control of government; thus, groups might fight to reverse a policy change enacted by a hostile prior government if they feel that they now have the power to do so (Stokes 2020: chap. 2). And if the constituency is already highly organized and strongly united in support of benefits under the status quo ante, they may be willing to refight a battle previously lost. Finally, if the constituency believes that key provisions of a policy are vulnerable to a legal challenge or to another challenge that can be mounted at a reasonable cost in a different venue than where the change at t_1 was originally enacted, they may also be more willing to challenge it (Stokes 2020: chap. 2).

Constituency pressures may also be complex and cross-cutting as well as unidirectional. The politically popular Medicare program for the elderly and disabled in the United States, for example, has largely avoided highly visible cutbacks to benefits for its core beneficiary groups, but initiatives to expand its coverage to a broader swath of the US population have faced strong opposition from health insurance companies, whose customer base it would take away. Thus, it has not provided a pathway to universal or quasi-universal coverage, as some of its supporters had hoped.

Mass Attitudes. If the constituency power feedback mechanism focuses on benefits and costs that are felt in a concentrated fashion by specific groups, the mass attitudes mechanism focuses on the perceptions of the broader public. But it also focuses on partisan elites, the media, and (increasingly) social media, who frame and prime public perceptions. If a policy provides widespread benefits, and those clients are perceived as deserving – or perhaps, more importantly, as *not un*deserving – then that program is likely to be of relatively low salience to the mass public. It is therefore not likely to undergo significant challenge and may perhaps also enjoy incremental growth if it also has a supportive core constituency. Indeed, low levels of partisan attachment among the electorate and polarization among party elites "could ensure a policy's survival irrespective of a party's immediate electoral fortunes and eventually provide a political foundation for future program growth" (Hacker and Pierson 2019: 14). Mettler and SoRelle (2018: 104) take the argument one step further, arguing that policies may build devoted electoral constituencies for the parties that enacted them, "thus turning those parties into devoted defenders" and helping both the parties and the policies to stay in place. Galvin and Thurston (2017: 334), on the other hand, claim that "the intellectual basis for thinking that policies are good vehicles for building electoral majorities – or good substitutes for the more tedious work of organizational party-building – is quite thin" and that "policies do not always, or even very often, generate their own political supports . . . [and] even when they do, there is little reason to think they will cement partisan loyalties." Hacker and Pierson (2019: 20) also argue that, at least for the United States in the current era of high polarization and low trust in government, "relying on public opinion to institutionalize a new program is unlikely to be a sufficient strategy in most domains."

Self-reinforcing politics through the mass politics mechanism can be challenged in several ways, notably by high salience focusing events that trigger program failures and undermine confidence in a program. Even in the absence of such focusing events, engagement by high-profile political and opinion leaders who have electoral incentives to frame a program as loss-imposing or flawed, or the constituency served by the program as undeserving, can undermine mass public support for a program. Moreover, the fact that political knowledge levels are low, and politics and policy are a sideshow for many citizens, gives elites lots of leeway for framing effects. A prominent example is the efforts of Republican leaders seeking to repeal the ACA (Weaver 2018). Such efforts are likely to be particularly common in periods of high partisan and ideological polarization, when political leaders may oppose policies to "differentiate themselves from their partisan opposition" (Lee 2009: 3; see also Patashnik 2019).

This self-undermining feedback mechanism also has inbuilt limitations, however: Downs' (1972) issue attention cycle suggests that public attention to an issue that does not have high innate salience will fade over time, as other issues capture the public's attention. Moreover, repeated failure of reform efforts may discourage leaders of countermobilizations from further investment in policy reform initiatives or at least they may become much more modest in their objectives.

4.3.3 Information, Attention, and Interpretation Mechanisms

While economic impacts and constituency power are important mechanisms for policy feedback, information – and how that information is interpreted and weighted – also plays a critical role in policy feedback. These mechanisms are of several types.

Information Mechanisms. Perhaps the most common-sense meaning of policy feedback is that policymakers, policy experts, and policy entrepreneurs inside and outside of government receive information about the efficacy and impacts of current government policies and programs and then consider policy revisions based on that information about its effects. This is the meaning stressed by John

Kingdon (1984) in his classic study of agenda-setting in the United States. Kingdon notes that this policy information comes in many forms and from multiple sources, each of which has its own potential for biases and imperfections. Sources of information include formal government reports, media and social media coverage, and inputs from citizens, interest groups, and policy evaluators. Of course, the type of information received, and the "spin" built into it, depends on factors such as how free the media and social media are and the resources that different interests must devote to conveying their preferred interpretation. This type of information can be used at any stage of the policy-making process but is likely to be especially important in agenda-setting, as governments decide which issues to address.

Elite Attention. A distinct but overlapping causal mechanism for policy feedback can be found in the PE intellectual tradition. In this approach, a key factor that constrains the range of issues that can get on a government's agenda is limitations on the capacity of political elites to pay attention to many issues simultaneously (see, e.g., Baumgartner and Jones 1993/2009; Baumgartner, Jones, and Mortensen 2018; Princen 2013). In addition, constituencies that benefit from the policy seek to develop "policy monopolies" that exclude outside voices from policy influence. Drawing on the Advocacy Coalition Framework (see, e.g., Jenkins-Smith et al. 2018), this approach also emphasizes the role of intellectual paradigms or policy ideas that are likely to reinforce the status quo and limit consideration of alternatives. While these stabilizing forces are occasionally subject to challenges and disruption, the general tendency is to return to the dominance of the policy status quo ante. As noted in Section 4.3.2, if policies are already in place that offer "half solutions" – imperfect solutions that nevertheless offer some response to a problem or problems – elites are likely to devote their limited attention to more immediately pressing problems (Campbell 2011).

Policy monopolies and dominant interpretive frameworks are not impervious to more serious challenges, however. Jones and Baumgartner (2005: 171) have noted that "the U.S. political system produces extreme allegiance to the status quo; interspersed with occasional frantic overreactions." Increased elite attention, and openness to alternative interpretive frameworks, is most likely when external shocks increase salience of the issue among the public and mobilize groups outside of the dominant policy coalition. Long periods of policy stability and major policy punctuations are thus seen as two sides of the same causal coin: "Radical shifts occur *because* some issues and negative consequences of existing policies are ignored in periods of policy stability. And policy change will be more radical to the extent that issues and problems have been ignored for a longer time" (Princen 2013: 855). Recent PE research has given increased attention to what PE theorists label "error accumulation" and how institutional arrangements may encourage or discourage efficient information processing (Chan and Zhao 2016; Lam and Chan 2015). Exogenous factors, notably weak institutional insulation of sectoral policymaking and the availability of alternative decision-making venues that have a legitimate claim to jurisdiction over the policy, increase the likelihood that a policy "punctuation" may occur. On the other hand, one study found that European Union policy change was less punctuated than in the United States because the "EU's legislative process is more isolated from public opinion than that in the US" (see the discussion in Princen 2013: 863), making it less susceptible to swings in public opinion.

Social Construction. In addition to the resources and political leverage of constituency groups, Schneider and Ingram (1993, 2005) have emphasized that the "social construction" of constituency groups is likely to influence their opportunities to both enact and maintain or expand policies that favor their interests. If program constituencies are "negatively constructed" in political discourse as "undeserving" of policies that provide benefits to them, those programs are more likely to experience pressures for retrenchment or even abolition. Schneider and Ingram point out that these social constructions are partially endogenous to policies; they may both reflect and reinforce how particular target populations are viewed. As noted in the previous section, benefits for military veterans and the aged in the United States both reflect societal perceptions that they are deserving of government aid and give them increased resources to ensure a continuing flow of benefits (Campbell 2003; Mettler 2005). Yet these self-reinforcing effects are by no means absolute. When programs gain a reputation as inefficient, corrupt, or patronage-ridden, as with Civil War veterans' pensions in the United States, they can undermine the positive social construction of both the program and its clientele (Skocpol 1992). Program characteristics can reinforce these social constructions and hence self-reinforcing effects; thus, social insurance programs (e.g., Social Security in the United States and public pension programs in many other countries) benefit in their social construction from being financed in whole or in part from employer and/or employee contributions, even when benefits received are disproportionate to contributions.

Negative constructions can also be created by public policies; Schneider and Ingram (2005: 5) argue, for example, that policy "can create categories – such as drunk drivers – which without the force of law would not have existed or at least would not have born any real stigma." Conscious or unconscious public associations between stigmatized groups such as racial minorities can lead to self-undermining effects for programs associated with those groups, as Martin

Gilens (1999) argued in *Why Americans Hate Welfare*. This is especially so when specific programs are identified with negative stereotypes of those groups' behavior (e.g., laziness). And when both resource and social construction effects reinforce each other, the consequences for marginalized populations can be severe. This is particularly evident, Vesla Weaver and Amanda Geller (2019: 191) argue, in "contemporary policing practices and crime control policies [that] have tended to deter engagement, cement inequality, and confer adverse legal and political socialization [and] give rise to pitched asymmetries of power, emboldening groups who do not bear the direct adverse effects of policing and punishment and diminishing the power of those who do."

Menu Contraction and Expansion. A closely related process to the sociopolitical policy feedback mechanisms concerns the "menu" of policy options that are actively considered as alternatives to the status quo. As policies become more "mature," the political and budgetary transition costs of major policy shifts grow, and the potential set of alternatives is likely to shift to incremental program fixes.

A process of continuous self-reinforcement and menu-narrowing is not foreordained, however. If the policy status quo produces concentrated losers, for example, those groups have an incentive to bear the search costs of developing potential alternatives. If incremental policy "patches" have been implemented but fail to address perceived policy problems that are seen as serious rather than an acceptable "cost of doing business," it may prompt a search for more transformative policy options or simply termination of the policy. And if multiple sources of policy expertise exist rather than expertise being concentrated in a narrow, cohesive, and self-protective policy elite, a more robust set of policy alternatives is likely to be generated (Jacobs and Weaver 2015). But whether that search succeeds in producing policy change depends in large part on whether viable plausible models for policy regime transition exist or can be created. Where they cannot, policy reform may make it to the policy agenda without resulting in formal policy change. In 2017, for example, the Trump administration's efforts to "repeal and replace" (or simply repeal) the Obama administration's Affordable Care Act fell just short in large part because they could not agree on an alternative that would not result in twenty million or more Americans losing their health care coverage.

4.3.4 Fiscal Mechanisms

Fiscal feedback mechanisms that can affect future rounds of policymaking or implementation are of two basic types, relating to whether a program has an earmarked financing mechanism and to the potential for "crowding out" by existing spending commitments.

Earmarked Revenue Sources. The former relates primarily to whether a program has an earmarked financing source. Programs with a dedicated revenue stream that provides adequate funding for the foreseeable future and does not place demands on general revenues are likely to receive limited attention and concern by budget guardians (e.g., budget offices and treasury ministries) and may be less subject to competing budgetary pressures during periods of economic austerity. Hence the effects are usually self-reinforcing and occur primarily at the agenda-setting stage. Yet, as Eric Patashnik (1997: 432) has noted, "collective promises may strengthen or weaken over time, but are nearly always subject to periodic renewal and renegotiation." Moreover, even trust fund financed programs that are self-financing in the short and medium term are likely to raise strong concerns among budget guardians if program expenditures are large and growing rapidly. A difficult overall fiscal climate may also prompt efforts to "raid" trust funds (Rabe and Hampton 2016).

Earmarked revenue sources may also have self-undermining feedback effects, moreover, in at least two distinct ways. First, if a program is financed only through earmarked revenues, with no general revenues permitted to be expended on the program, insufficient dedicated funding to meet program commitments may spark a "trust fund crisis" in which expenditures are automatically reduced unless policymakers intervene (Pierson 1994: 173–174). Such trust fund crises helped to prompt Social Security reform legislation in the United States in both 1977 and 1983 (Weaver 1988; Béland 2005), as well as in the Medicare program (Oberlander 2003: chap. 4). Program financing mechanisms may also lead to program cutbacks without a trust fund crisis: Some programs – notably in the public pension sector – contain automatic stabilizing mechanisms that reduce program commitments gradually based on projected (or sometimes current) budgetary, economic, and demographic trends. In public pension programs, for example, such mechanisms can lead to automatic benefit cuts or increases in the standard retirement age without intervention by policymakers – and if they can resist political incentives to intervene (Weaver 2016). Recent assessments suggest that such automatic stabilizing mechanisms do have some effect in changing policy outputs and outcomes at t_2, but that where such mechanisms are poorly insulated from control by politicians, they are vulnerable to erosion or reversal (Weaver 2016). Trust funds can also be subject to external shocks – for example, the growth in auto fuel efficiency standards and increase in use of electric vehicles can lead to declines in transportation trust funds funded by motor fuel taxation if the tax rates are not adjusted over time (Perl and Burke 2018).

Crowding Out. Even in the absence of a trust fund mechanism, fiscal conditions that are either program-specific or related to a country's overall fiscal situation may affect later program decisions. Morgan and Campbell (2011), for example, argue that rapid Medicare expenditure growth in the United States after 1965 both undermined the framers' plans for an incremental path to universal health insurance and thwarted any push for the expansion of basic Medicare benefits package until addition of prescription drugs in the 2003 Medicare Modernization Act. More generally, economic downturns and slower economic growth increase the pressure from budget guardians for expenditure reductions, and the heavy expenditure burden of entitlement program expenditures for the elderly may "crowd out" expenditures for new social risks and program initiatives for other vulnerable populations.

4.3.5 State Capacity and Administrative Mechanisms

Very few policies are completely self-implementing; most require some detailed procedures and usually an organizational apparatus to put them into effect. Thus, as Moynihan and Soss (2014: 320) argue, "bureaucracies are not only creatures but also creators of the political forces that impinge on them," and "administrative organizations are, in their own right, sites of politics." But this is essentially to say that implementation is a political process (the left-hand side of Figure 3); it does not necessarily involve policy feedback in the sense of changes in policy choices, outputs, or outcomes at a later stage.

Recent research does suggest several types of state capacity and administrative feedback mechanisms with important implications for later polity stasis and change. A first type, which Isabel Perera (2021a, 2021b) has labeled "supply-side policy feedbacks," can be considered an extension of the "Constituency Resources and Power" mechanism outlined in Section 4.3.2, but with the *providers* of the policy rather than its recipients as the key constituencies. These providers may include both agency leadership and the "program operators" (Wilson 1991) who deliver the program, either directly through government agencies or through nongovernmental entities (e.g., private sector physicians, for-profit providers of government-guaranteed mortgages or student loans).

Supply-side feedbacks from administrators and providers do not always support policy and program expansion, however. Administering agencies may sometimes be hostile to a policy: Jake Haselswerdt (2014: 753) argues that the greater susceptibility of older tax breaks to elimination than older spending programs in the United States may be due in part to weak administrative champions for the latter: "older spending programs are more likely to have a large, entrenched, and politically organized staff with relationships on Capitol Hill, but Treasury Department bureaucrats disdain tax expenditures of all ages." Probably more typical is the situation described by Morgan and Campbell

(2011): In a "delegated welfare state" with a strong role for private providers, those providers may provide additional allies for a policy's creation and are unlikely to be actively hostile to a program, but they may be opposed to further expansion of a program if it they believe that doing so means losing autonomy in the way they operate or a less generous financing arrangement, as has historically been the case with physicians in the United States with the expansion of government-provided health insurance. How and how well providers are organized can also affect their ability to press for types of program expansions they favor and block program retrenchment or transformation that they oppose (Perera 2020, 2021b). Having strong political leverage (e.g., teachers unions in off-cycle elections in the United States) can also mediate the strength of providers' influence on subsequent policy (Anzia 2011).

Policy-induced administrative feedback mechanisms can also take the form of a *means/ends match or mismatch*. When the agency administering a policy has a clear and achievable mandate, along with the financial resources, technical capacity, and an administrative structure that allow it to achieve policy goals, as well as an organizational mission that causes it to prioritize the policy, it is more likely to avoid visible policy failures that prompt the public and generalist policymakers to reassess the program and the agency's management of it. The design of a policy also matters, notably the degree to which multiple policy "instruments, sequenced and assembled in 'portfolios' or 'bundles', work in concert to give effect to different aspects of a policy goal" (Bali, Capano, and Ramesh 2019: 3). Of course, characteristics of the policy can make this more likely – for example, being a relatively simple set of tasks that are consistent with implementing agency skills and resources, and simple administrative arrangements requiring minimal cooperation of actors with conflicting goals. These conditions are likely to create self-reinforcing feedback effects. On the other hand, a means/ends mismatch is likely to involve a mismatch of agency mission and resources with program responsibilities, leading to visible failures that in turn damage the administering agency's and program's external reputation and political support. This is particularly true if those failures recur frequently and grow in visibility or appear to get worse.

Multilevel governance arrangements, notably federalism, can shape both "supply-side" policy feedbacks and policy match/mismatch feedbacks. Because federal arrangements and the policy dynamics they give rise to vary widely (Weaver 2020), it is difficult to generalize about how multilevel governance interacts with feedback effects, but several effects are evident in the literature. Karch and Rose (2017), for example, argue that an alliance of state officials and business interests in the United States has been resistant to nationalizing eligibility and benefit levels in the Unemployment Insurance program created in 1935 because it gave states more control over the program and facilitated a "race to the bottom" favored by powerful business interests. More generally, a program structure that gives second-level governments discretion over important program provisions may lead to differences in those programs that reflect differences in ideology, party control, and fiscal capacity across those governmental units (Fording and Patton 2020; Weaver 2020). It may even lead to the growth of regional identities that shape future policy development (Béland and Lecours 2020).

4.4 Considering Feedback Mechanisms in Context

The discussion in this section has focused thus far on identifying the great range of feedback mechanisms and effects affecting policy stasis and change that appear in the literature to facilitate the development of clear, specific hypotheses that can inform future research. It is equally important, however, to recognize that these feedback mechanisms are often intertwined and mutually reinforcing.

Equally important, efforts to identify feedback mechanisms that affect policy stasis and change and are generalizable *across* policy sectors and societies and over time should not be made at the cost of downplaying critical interactions of feedback mechanisms and partially exogenous conditions that are *specific* to concrete sectors, societies, and time periods. Most important, policy feedback research must pay increased attention to the interaction of social divisions and policy feedback mechanisms when those social divisions involve strong differences in group power, have policy effects that are persistent over time and pervasive across policy sectors, and are reinforced by social constructions and administrative arrangements. In the United States, for example, Hacker and Pierson (2019: 13) have argued that we must update our understanding of feedback mechanisms that have "focused on historical periods in which partisan cleavages were far less prominent than they are today," especially if those assessments are to be used to provide advice for current policymakers. Jamila Michener (2019: 425) argues that in the United States, "public policy is one of the primary institutional purveyors of racial inequity" (see also Rosenthal 2021; Thurston 2018). The distributive, exclusionary, and social construction effects of Jim Crow laws in the United States are merely the most obvious examples of racialized policymaking in the United States that created long-term self-reinforcing feedbacks – but ultimately self-undermining ones as well. Other examples include highway construction policy, home ownership, and local land use regulations (see, e.g., Thurston 2015). In Canada, the intertwining of regional-economic and regional-linguistic divisions with political institutions and policy feedback has been similarly fundamental in shaping policy stasis and change (Béland and Lecours 2020), as have caste and religion in India.

4.5 Policy Feedback in Authoritarian Regimes

Thus far in this Element, we have concentrated on the effect of the impact of policy feedback mechanisms in democratic or quasi-democratic regimes – that is, regimes where feedback mechanisms that take public opinions into account (1) are at least potentially impactful on decisions by political leaders and (2) are less subject to manipulation and control by those political leaders. We turn now briefly to feedback mechanisms and feedback effects in authoritarian regimes, with the caveat that this is a very under-researched topic.

It is important to note at the outset that authoritarian regimes are an incredibly diverse category, ranging from traditional hereditary monarchies like Saudi Arabia to military regimes and to single-party systems like China with highly developed and intricate political institutions. They share some common characteristics in varying degrees – a lack of free and fair contestation of elections; limitations on freedoms of speech, association, and media; and weak (or nonexistent) institutionalized checks on governing elites – but otherwise are very diverse (see, e.g., Geddes 1999). Moreover, authoritarianism versus democracy is a continuum rather than two easily distinguishable bins into which all countries can be neatly sorted (Levitsky and Way 2010).

Taking all these caveats into consideration, there are some processes that are likely to be similar between authoritarian and democratic regimes, particularly with respect to increasing return mechanisms. Transition costs to a new policy in authoritarian regimes are still likely to be high in many policy sectors due to coordination, learning, and adaptation effects. Many authoritarian governments worry to some extent about their maintaining support from key groups who benefit from current policies of the current regime and help keep it in power, although in authoritarian regimes these groups are more likely to be military and economic – and in some cases party – elites rather than the public at large. These groups may be able to entrench themselves further the longer supportive political elites hold power, just as interests in competitive regimes do. And most authoritarian governments do worry to some extent about their legitimacy with the public, even if they do not have to worry about losing elections: Greater legitimacy means that they do not have to rule through pure repression.

Yet authoritarian regimes also have some critical differences from democratic regimes, although overgeneralization about this very diverse set of regimes should be avoided. Because most of these regimes do not face strong electoral threats (or in single-party regimes, any electoral threats at all), and they may have both greater capacity and greater willingness to stifle political opposition that arises when change imposes costs, many authoritarian regimes may be more willing to bear the economic and social costs of changing policies. Authoritarian governance also poses some unique challenges: Because of restrictions on the media and lower-level officials' fear of delivering bad news, top leadership may not get adequate upward flow of information to facilitate early adaptation and fixing of negative policy effects (Wallace 2016). Authoritarian leaders are also likely to have greater capacity to hide losses when they *are* aware of them and use the media and social media to shape how much information is presented and how it is presented. In the case of the famines resulting from the Great Leap Forward mobilization campaign in China, for example, all the above factors – failure to transmit negative information upward, ignoring or downplaying information that was received, leadership at the top proceeding with policies that were known to have great costs, and lower-down officials trying to remain in the good graces of capricious leaders at the top – are evident (see, e.g., Bernstein 2006; Chan 2001).

Several studies of policy feedback in authoritarian regimes offer insights into these mechanisms. Not surprisingly, some studies focus on informational feedback mechanisms. In the highly institutionalized authoritarian regime of Singapore, for example, where partisan competition is allowed within strict limits and both press and associational freedom are restricted, the party-state has instituted several consultation mechanisms to influence "who can participate, how, and on what" (Rodan 2018: 93), while ensuring that such participation remained "constructive" and within acceptable bounds. An "informational feedback" system of experimentation, learning, and policy revision is given much of the credit for the success of China's economic reforms beginning in the 1980s (see, e.g., Cai and Treisman 2006; Leutert 2021). At the same time, however, deficiencies and widespread gaming in the Target-Based Responsibility System show that the accurate gathering of information by the central party-state still incurs major problems (Gao 2015, 2016). Scholars in the PE tradition argue that "Punctuated equilibrium emerges in authoritarian states because officials have poor exposure to information, which undermines their ability and incentive to make frequent adjustments to the status quo. At the same time, authoritarian institutions allow decision makers to undertake radical changes unopposed when they become alerted to signals indicating threats to regime survival" (Chan and Zhao 2016: 148). The provision of concentrated benefits to interests (notably large state enterprises in China and oligarchic cronies in Putin's Russia) that they can use to reinforce their positions are other examples of self-reinforcing policy feedbacks that are characteristic of authoritarian regimes, though the risk of losing their privileged position (and worse) by running afoul of political leaders is almost certainly higher in many authoritarian regimes than in most democracies.

4.6 Conclusions and Research Directions

This discussion suggests several important conclusions about the impacts of policy feedback on policy change. A first conclusion is that claims about policy feedback effects should be careful to specify both the dimensions of those effects (direction, temporality, etc.) and the specific causal mechanism(s) and facilitating or limiting conditions that underlie them. Given the multidimensionality of feedback effects on policy change, generalized claims about policy feedback effects on later policy change are as likely to mislead as to add to knowledge.

Second, analyses that focus on policy feedback mechanisms and effects should consider both self-reinforcing and self-undermining feedbacks, which "frequently flow simultaneously from the same set of policies" (Jacobs and Weaver 2015: 454), as well as the interaction between the two. This is not to say that the two are equal in their prevalence or their impact; even researchers who stress the importance of self-undermining feedbacks generally agree that, most of the time, in most policy sectors, self-reinforcing feedbacks are likely to dominate. But self-undermining feedbacks are likely to play a major role in setting the *agenda* for potential policy reforms as well as explaining "*why* change emerged; self-reinforcing effects, meanwhile, will often offer a compelling account of why reform takes the specific *form* that it does" (Jacobs and Weaver 2015: 454; italics in original).

Three additional conclusions need to be considered together: the conditional nature of policy feedback mechanisms and effects, the potential variation in the strength of the feedback mechanisms, and the difficulty of separating endogenous policy-originated causes from the exogenous societal context in which a policy is set. These are represented in the fourth and fifth columns of Table 2. Not all policies are the same in their parameters. Transition costs to a new policy regime or in the degree to which policies create immediate and concentrated flows of benefits to specific constituencies vary widely across sectors and specific policy choices, for example (see column 4 of Table 2). And these clearly interact with at least partially exogenous factors such as the strength and unity of constituency groups, the ideology of the political party(ies) in power, and the strength and number of political system veto points in determining how particular causal mechanisms operate (see column 5 of Table 2). Overall, this suggests that very broad statements such as "universalistic social programs are more resilient than means-tested ones in resisting austerity pressures" should almost always be hedged in at least two ways: by specifying the causal mechanism(s) that underlie the causal claim and by specifying the mediating conditions under which the causal mechanism is likely to operate in a strong (or unmuted) form and those under which it is less likely to hold.

A sixth conclusion flows partially from the prior three: Policy feedback mechanisms are generally not a *sufficient* cause of either policy stasis or change (Oberlander and Weaver 2015: 44). As both Kingdon's Multiple Streams Framework (Herweg, Zahariadis, and Zohlnhöfer 2018) and the Advocacy Coalition Framework suggest, political opportunities that arise predictably (e.g., a change in party control of government) or unpredictably (e.g., a negative focusing event) play a major role in determining whether formal policy change makes it to governments' policy agendas, and what happens if they do.

This review of the relationship between policy feedback and policy change also suggests some useful directions for future research. One area where expanded research effort is needed is in understanding the conditions under which feedback mechanisms are likely to be weak or nonexistent, building on the pioneering work of Patashnik (2008; see also Patashnik and Zelizer 2013). As noted in Section 4.4, Hacker and Pierson have expressed skepticism about the impact of mass public opinion on creating self-reinforcing feedback in an era of high polarization and low trust in government; whether the same is true in other societies remains under-researched.

A second area where further research is needed is in coverage of a broader range of policy sectors and countries. In the HI tradition in particular, early work on policy feedback was concentrated in social policy beginning with the work of Skocpol and Pierson and continuing with work by Béland, Campbell, Mettler, and others. The explicit use of policy feedback terminology and frameworks has diffused to other policy sectors, notably energy and the environment, but research on other policy sectors has often used concepts that are consistent with the policy feedback mechanisms and effects discussed here without explicit mention of the policy feedback literature. The same is true of research on the effects of policy feedback on policy stasis and change outside of the United States. More of such research is needed, especially explicitly comparative cross-national research (for examples, see e.g., Hacker 1998; Karapin 2014; Perera 2021b).

5 From Theory to Practice: Policy Feedback and Policy Design

Both scholars and policy practitioners are increasingly concerned with using research findings about policy feedback to "find practical answers to long-term policy challenges" (Sewerin, Béland, and Cashore 2020: 243) and inform policy design to ensure that those policies are better able to achieve their objectives. Is it possible to design "policies that intentionally stick" (Jordan and Matt 2014) or are "sustainable" (Patashnik and Weaver 2021) rather than being vulnerable to retrenchment or reversal? Equally important, recent scholarship stresses that policy sustainability should not be confused with policy *rigidity*. Instead, the goal should be "'dynamic' policy effectiveness, i.e., ensuring that the policy addresses not only the problem in each context, but how it adapts to changing conditions and circumstances over time" (Bali, Capano, and Ramesh 2019: 3), allowing the policy to "continue to deliver, over time, their intended functions, purposes and objectives, even under negative circumstances" (Howlett, Capano, and Ramesh 2018: 415). Patashnik and Weaver (2021), for example, have developed a set of potential threats to policy sustainability, a set of "warning signs" that can be used to assess the degree of threat, and a set of strategies for increasing sustainability.

Much of the policy design literature on policy feedback has a strong normative undertone, defining the challenge as designing and implementing "reforms" that will be sustainable and able to withstand attacks by their opponents. The Policy Feedback Project spearheaded by Jacob Hacker and Paul Pierson (2019), for instance, seeks strategies to overcome partisan polarization and institutional gridlock in the United States and examine "how *policy* might remake American politics" to "actively address a set of fundamental challenges, including climate change and the strains facing our health care and criminal justice systems" as well as counteracting actions by "*critics* of such active policies [who] have themselves proved adept at using policy to achieve their own preferred ends – often at the state level" (Hacker and Pierson 2019: 11). Hacker and Pierson (2019: 12) describe a changing US political system in which policies in sectors such as pensions and health care for the elderly

> that began as ambitious and risky undertakings evolved to achieve the status of political "third rails." ... In area after area, federal policies that once sparked controversy came to be taken for granted ... The long arc of history appeared to bend toward successful policy feedback that supported an active "Big Government." In recent years, however, advocates of active government have seemed less capable of generating such self-reinforcing effects.

In a period of high partisan polarization, it is less likely that voters will "view the other party's proposals sympathetically on *any* prominent issue. This has made it much more difficult to gain broad acceptance for new initiatives that might traditionally have been expected to have strong positive feedback effects" (Hacker and Pierson 2019: 14). While the particulars of polarization and increased inequality may limit the generalizability of this argument beyond the United States, Hacker and Pierson's analysis does suggest that understanding country-specific contexts for policy feedback will be critical to efforts to integrate feedback mechanisms into policy design.

Proponents of increased action to address climate change have been another important set of advocates for incorporating research on policy feedback into policy design (see, e.g., Rosenbloom, Meadowcroft, and Cashore 2019). Their efforts suggest that detailed analysis of policy mechanisms in a specific *policy sector* can offer rich rewards, given the common problems in climate change policy of developing policies to address a problem that has a gradual onset, has powerful beneficiaries from the status quo, and requires substantial investments, learning, coordination, and adaptive expectations from multiple stakeholders to achieve policy objectives. As part of this analysis, it is important to recognize that those seeking to promote policy change may have to undo the effects of accumulated self-reinforcing policy feedbacks that tend to entrench the policy status quo.

In this brief concluding section, we examine the issue of policy design by building on the discussion in Section 3 on policy feedback and mass politics and in Section 4 on how policy feedback mechanisms affect policy stasis and change. We begin by discussing potential strategies for policy design that can be used by political actors seeking to reinforce or undermine the sustainability of specific policies. We then discuss constraints on the use of policy design to promote or undermine policy sustainability.

5.1 Feedback Mechanisms and Policy Design

What does the analysis of the policy feedback mechanisms discussed in Sections 3 and 4 suggest in terms of strategies that can be used to inform strategic decisions by political actors seeking to employ self-reinforcing or self-undermining policy feedback mechanisms? We draw on the analysis in Section 4 regarding (1) the existence of both self-reinforcing and self-undermining mechanisms, (2) the conditionality of policy feedback mechanisms, and (3) the intertwining of policy feedbacks and "exogenous" contextual factors that vary widely across political systems and policy sectors. We also draw on Hacker and Pierson's (2019: 21) fundamental insight that policy-makers and other political actors need to think strategically "in a dynamic fashion – to think about establishment, entrenchment, and expansion, as well as enactment" – and that this advice holds for actors seeking to retrench, transform, or abolish policies, as well as those seeking to entrench them.

Table 3 outlines a series of strategies focused on each of the self-reinforcing and self-undermining feedback mechanisms discussed in Section 4, including both strategies to strengthen (indicated with a "+") and weaken ("–") the operation of that mechanism. Initiatives to take advantage of concentrated

Table 3 Feedback strategies

Mechanism Type with Main Causal Mechanism	Strategies to Strengthen (+) or Weaken (−) Feedback Mechanism
ECONOMIC RETURNS	
Increasing Returns	+ Subsidize transition costs for key stakeholders to lower their learning and coordination costs and reset adaptive expectations until adaptation is complete
Diminishing or Static Returns	+ Subsidize transition costs for new policy proposals for key stakeholders to lower their learning and coordination costs and reset adaptive expectations
	+ Concentrate on reform proposals with low transition costs
SOCIOPOLITICAL	
Concentrated Constituency Benefits and Resources, or	+ Frontload concentrated program benefits and backload program costs
	+ Diffuse losses or compensate losers until policy is firmly entrenched
	+ Provide resources to constituency groups who benefit as part of policy
Concentrated Constituency Losses:	+ Organize and mobilize constituency groups who are harmed by policy
Mass Public and Party Support, or	+ Frame policy as beneficial to society
Mass Public and Party Opposition	+ Frame issue as harmful to society and increase issue salience
Elite Attention Overload, or	+ Lower policy visibility through stealth policy mechanisms (e.g., tax expenditures)
Punctuated Attention	+ Highlight and frame policy failures when they occur
	+ Push policy change through quickly while public attention is high
	− Stall policy action until public attention declines
INFORMATIONAL/INTERPRETIVE	
Information	− Conceal negative information about policy failures
Positive Social Construction	+ Frame program constituency as deserving of policy benefits

Table 3 (cont.)

Mechanism Type with Main Causal Mechanism	Strategies to Strengthen (+) or Weaken (−) Feedback Mechanism
Negative Social Construction	+ Frame program constituency as undeserving of program benefits or deserving of program penalties
Menu Contraction, or	+ Restrict funding to study shortcomings of current policy and potential alternatives
Menu Expansion	+ Support organizations that provide research on policy alternatives
FISCAL	
Earmarked Financing, or	+ Assign earmarked revenue source to program that is adequate to finance it for foreseeable future
	+ Allow general revenue financing as backstop for program in case of unexpected revenue shortfalls
Trust Fund Crisis and Automatic Stabilizing Mechanisms	+ Prohibit general revenue inputs into program
STATE CAPACITY AND ADMINISTRATIVE ARRANGEMENTS	
Self-Reinforcing Supply-Side Feedbacks	+ Assign implementation responsibility for program to agencies whose mission is complementary to its objectives
Self-Undermining Supply-Side Feedbacks	+ Assign implementation responsibility for program to agencies hostile or indifferent to its objectives
Means/Ends Match	+ Provide adequate supply of funding, expertise, etc.
	+ Simplify administrative arrangements
Means/Ends Mismatch	+ Deny adequate funds to program to achieve objectives

constituency benefits, for example, might frontload those benefits in their proposals, as well as simultaneously assigning administrative responsibility for the program to an agency with a closely aligned mission, while keeping its tasks and administrative structure relatively simple and ensuring that it was supplied with adequate financial and technical resources. Interests seeking to block such an initiative or prevent its entrenchment might seek to frontload concentrated costs.

5.2 Constraints on Incorporating Policy Feedback into Policy Design

Research also suggests several important constraints on efforts to design "resilient," "sustainable," or even expanding policies using feedback mechanisms, however. First, policies at t_1 are rarely written on blank slates; they are instead frequently meshed with or layered on top of existing policies that have their own constituencies, distributions of costs and benefits, and legitimations. Unless compromises are made in creating new policies to protect the constituents of prior policies, proposals for policy change may not be adopted. But those compromises may lead to policy inconsistencies or to pledges that cannot be kept, as in President Obama's pledge that those who like their current insurance would be able to keep it after enactment of the 2010 Patient Protection and ACA in the United States.

Second, as Béland, Rocco, and Waddan (2016: 204) have noted, many societal changes that interact with and shape policy feedback mechanisms are not anticipated at the time programs are created, especially when those programs have been in place for a long time. But if social changes are not anticipated, they are unlikely to be addressed in policy design. Except in political systems where a cohesive political executive monopolizes the policymaking and policy implementation process for an extended period, there is a risk that compromises will need to be made as a policy is adopted and implemented that will undermine its political, financial, or administrative sustainability.

Third, individual strategies each have their own limitations. Building strong constituency support for a program in its vulnerable early years may involve efforts to "frontload" (i.e., put in place immediately) concentrated benefits and "backload" concentrated costs, for example. But such initiatives may be constrained in some countries by fiscal rules that limit spending that is not offset by increased revenues or other spending reductions, as the case of the ACA in the United States illustrates (Oberlander and Weaver 2015: 44).

As this discussion suggests, not all feedback strategies will be available in every case. Nor is reliance on shaping feedback mechanisms the best investment of scarce resources for political actors trying to shape future policy; some more general strategies, such as venue-shopping to find the most favorable arena for decision-making, may be more effective. Strategies to incorporate policy feedback mechanisms into policy design are nevertheless likely to be a part of the repertoire of many political actors in the years ahead. This is something policy feedback researchers should keep in mind moving forward.

References

Amenta, E. (1998) *Bold Relief: Institutional Politics and the Origins of Modern Social Policy* (Princeton, NJ: Princeton University Press).

Anzia, S. F. (2011) Election Timing and the Electoral Influence of Interest Groups, *The Journal of Politics* 73(2), 412–427.

Arnold, R. D. (1990) *The Logic of Congressional Action* (New Haven, CT: Yale University Press).

Arthur, W. B. (1989) Competing Technologies, Increasing Returns, and Lock-In by Historical Events, *The Economic Journal*, 99(394), 116–131.

Ashok, V. L. and G. A. Huber (2020) Do Means of Program Delivery and Distributional Consequences Affect Policy Support? Experimental Evidence about the Sources of Citizens' Policy Opinions, *Political Behavior* 42(4), 1097–1118.

Baicker, K. and A. Finkelstein (2019) The Impact of Medicaid Expansion on Voter Participation: Evidence from the Oregon Health Insurance Experiment, *Quarterly Journal of Political Science* 14(4), 383–400.

Bali, A. S., G. Capano, and M. Ramesh (2019) Anticipating and Designing for Policy Effectiveness, *Policy and Society* 38(1), 1–13.

Barnes, C. Y. (2020) *State of Empowerment: Low-Income Families and the New Welfare State* (Ann Arbor: University of Michigan Press).

Barnes, C. Y. and E. C. Hope (2017) Means-Tested Public Assistance Programs and Adolescent Political Socialization, *Journal of Youth and Adolescence* 46 (7), 1611–1621.

Baumgartner, F., C. Breunig, C. Green-Pedersen et al. (2009) Punctuated Equilibrium in Comparative Perspective, *American Journal of Political Science* 53(3), 603–620.

Baumgartner, F. R. and B. D. Jones (1993/2009) *Agendas and Instability in American Politics* (Chicago: University of Chicago Press).

Baumgartner, F. R. and B. D. Jones (2002) Positive and Negative Feedback in Politics. In F. R. Baumgartner and B. D. Jones, eds., *Policy Dynamics* (Chicago: University of Chicago Press), 3–28.

Baumgartner, F. R., B. D. Jones, and P. Mortensen (2018) Punctuated Equilibrium Theory: Explaining Stability and Change in Public Policy. In C. Weible and P. Sabatier, eds., *Theories of the Policy Process*, 4th ed. (New York: Routledge), 55–102.

Béland, D. (2005) *Social Security: History and Politics from the New Deal to the Privatization Debate* (Lawrence: University Press of Kansas).

Béland, D. (2007) Ideas and Institutional Change in Social Security: Conversion, Layering, and Policy Drift, *Social Science Quarterly* 88(1), 20–38.

Béland, D. (2010) Reconsidering Policy Feedback: How Policies Affect Politics, *Administration and Society* 42(5), 568–590.

Béland, D. and B. Gran, eds. (2008) *Public and Private Social Policy: Health and Pension Policies in a New Era* (Basingstoke: Palgrave Macmillan).

Béland, D. and J. S. Hacker (2004) Ideas, Private Institutions, and American Welfare State "Exceptionalism": The Case of Health and Old-Age Insurance, 1915–1965, *International Journal of Social Welfare*, 13(1), 42–54.

Béland, D., M. Howlett, P. Rocco, and A. Waddan (2020) Designing Policy Resilience: Lessons from the Affordable Care Act, *Policy Sciences*, 53(2), 243–252.

Béland, D. and A. Lecours (2020) Ideas, Federalism, and Policy Feedback: An Institutionalist Approach, *Territory, Politics, Governance*. https://doi.org/10.1080/21622671.2020.1837225TS: Link.

Béland, D., P. Rocco, and A. Waddan (2016) Reassessing Policy Drift: Social Policy Change in the United States, *Social Policy and Administration* 50(2), 201–218.

Béland, D., P. Rocco, and A. Waddan (2019) Policy Feedback and the Politics of the Affordable Care Act, *Policy Studies Journal* 47(2), 395–422.

Béland, D. and E. Schlager, eds. (2019a) Policy Feedback in Public Policy Research, Special Issue, *Policy Studies Journal* 27(2), 179–491.

Béland, D. and E. Schlager (2019b) Varieties of Policy Feedback Research: Looking Backward, Moving Forward, *Policy Studies Journal* 47(2), 184–205.

Bell, E. (2020) The Politics of Designing Tuition-Free College: How Socially Constructed Target Populations Influence Policy Support, *Journal of Higher Education* 91(6), 888–926.

Berkowitz, E. D. (2003) *Robert Ball and the Politics of Social Security* (Madison: University of Wisconsin Press).

Bernstein, T. P. (2006) Mao Zedong and the Famine of 1959–1960: Study in Willfulness, *China Quarterly* 186, 421–445.

Berry, C., D. Burden, and W. Howell (2010) After Enactment: The Lives and Deaths of Federal Programs, *American Journal of Political Science* 54(1), 1–17.

Bol, D., G. Marco, A. Blais, and P. J. Loewen (2021) The Effect of COVID-19 Lockdowns on Political Support: Some Good News for Democracy? *European Journal of Political Research* 60(2), 497–505.

Bonoli, G. (2001) Political Institutions, Veto Points, and the Process of Welfare State Adaptation. In P. Pierson, ed., *The New Politics of the Welfare State* (New York: Oxford University Press), 238–264.

Bowler, S., S. P. Nicholson, and G. M. Segura (2006) Earthquakes and Aftershocks: Race, Direct Democracy, and Partisan Change, *American Journal of Political Science* 50(1), 146–159.

Bruch, S. K., M. M. Ferree, and J. Soss (2010) From Policy to Polity: Democracy, Paternalism and the Incorporation of Disadvantaged Citizen, *American Sociological Review* 75(2), 205–226.

Burgin, E. (2018) Congress, Policy Sustainability, and the Affordable Care Act: Democratic Policy Makers Overlooked Implementation, Post-Enactment Politics, and Policy Feedback Effects, *Congress and the Presidency* 45(3), 279–314.

Busemeyer, M. R., A. Abrassart, and R. Nezi (2021) Beyond Positive and Negative: New Perspectives on Feedback Effects in Public Opinion on the Welfare State, *British Journal of Political Science* 51(1), 137–162.

Cai, H. and D. Treisman (2006) Did Government Decentralization Cause China's Economic Miracle?, *World Politics* 58(4), 505–535.

Campbell, A. L. (2003) *How Policies Make Citizens: Senior Political Activism and the American Welfare State* (Princeton, NJ: Princeton University Press).

Campbell, A. L. (2011) Policy Feedbacks and the Impact of Policy Designs on Public Opinion, *Journal of Health Politics, Policy and Law* 36(6), 961–973.

Campbell, A. L. (2012) Policies Make Mass Publics, *Annual Review of Political Science* 15, 333–351.

Campbell, J. L. (2004) *Institutional Change and Globalization* (Princeton, NJ: Princeton University Press).

Cates, J. R. (1983) *Insuring Inequality: Administrative Leadership in Social Security, 1935–1954* (Ann Arbor: University of Michigan Press).

Chan, A. (2001) *Mao's Crusade: Politics and Policy Implementation in China's Great Leap Forward* (Oxford: Oxford University Press).

Chan, K. N. and S. Zhao (2016), Punctuated Equilibrium and the Information Disadvantage of Authoritarianism: Evidence from the People's Republic of China, *Policy Studies Journal* 44(2), 134–155.

Chattopadhyay, J. (2017) Is the ACA's Dependent Coverage Provision Generating Positive Feedback Effects among Young Adults? *Poverty and Public Policy* 9(1), 42–70.

Clinton, J. D. and M. W. Sances (2018) The Politics of Policy: The Initial Mass Political Effects of Medicaid Expansion in the States, *American Political Science Review* 112(1), 167–185.

Cook, F. L. and E. J. Barrett (1992) *Support for the American Welfare State: The Views of Congress and the Public* (New York: Columbia University Press).

Cook, J. B., V. Kogan, S. Lavertu, and Z. Peskowitz (2020) Government Privatization and Political Participation: The Case of Charter Schools, *Journal of Politics* 82(1), 300–314.

Courtemanche, C., J. Marton, and A. Yelowitz (2020) The Full Impact of the Affordable Care Act on Political Participation, *RSF: The Russell Sage Foundation Journal of the Social Sciences* 6(2), 179–204.

Cruz Nichols, V., A. M. W. LeBrón, and F. I. Pedraza (2018) Spillover Effects: Immigrant Policing and Government Skepticism in Matters of Health for Latinos, *Public Administration Review* 78, 432–443.

Dagan, D. and S. M. Teles (2014) Locked In? Conservative Reform and the Future of Mass Incarceration, *The Annals of the American Academy of Political and Social Science* 651, 266–276.

Dagan, D. and S. M. Teles (2016) *Prison Break: Why Conservatives Turned Against Mass Incarceration* (Oxford: Oxford University Press).

Davenport, T. C. (2015) The Effect of a Son's Conscription Risk on the Voting Behavior of His Parents, *American Journal of Political Science* 59(1), 225–241.

De La O, A. L. (2013) Do Conditional Cash Transfers Affect Electoral Behavior? Evidence from a Randomized Experiment in Mexico, *American Journal of Political Science* 57(1), 1–14.

De Zwart, F. (2015) Unintended but Not Unanticipated Consequences, *Theory and Society* 44(3), 283–297.

Derthick, M. (1979) *Policymaking for Social Security* (Washington, DC: Brookings Institution).

Di Tella, R. S. Galiani, and E. Schargrodsky (2012) Reality versus Propaganda in the Formation of Beliefs about Privatization. *Journal of Public Economics* 96(5–6): 553–567.

Downs, A. (1972) Up and Down with Ecology: The Issue Attention Cycle, *The Public Interest* 32, 38–50.

Druckman, J. N., J. E. Rothschild, and E. A. Sharrow (2018) Gender Policy Feedback: Perceptions of Sex Equity, Title IX, and Political Mobilization among College Athletes, *Political Research Quarterly* 71(3), 642–653.

Dunn, J. (1978) The Importance of Being Earmarked: Transport Policy and Highway Finance in Great Britain and the United States, *Comparative Studies in Society and History* 20(1), 29–53.

Ellingsaeter, A. L., R. H. Kitterod, and J. Lyngstad (2017) Universalizing Childcare, Changing Mothers' Attitudes: Policy Feedback in Norway, *Journal of Social Policy* 46(1), 149–173.

Erikson, R. S., M. B. MacKuen, and J. A. Stimson (2002) *The Macro Polity* (New York: Cambridge University Press).

Esping-Andersen, G. (1990) *The Three Worlds of Welfare Capitalism* (Cambridge: Polity).

Evans, P. B., D. Rueschemeyer, and T. Skocpol, eds. (1985) *Bringing the State Back In* (New York: Cambridge University Press).

Fang, A. H. and G. A. Huber (2020) Perceptions of Deservingness and the Politicization of Social Insurance: Evidence from Disability Insurance in the United States, *American Politics Research* 48(5), 543–559.

Faricy, C. and C. Ellis (2014) Public Attitudes toward Social Spending in the United States: The Differences between Direct Spending and Tax Expenditures, *Political Behavior* 36(1), 53–76.

Fioretos, O., T. G. Falleti, and A. Sheingate, eds. (2016) *The Oxford Handbook of Historical Institutionalism* (Oxford: Oxford University Press).

Flavin, P. and M. T. Hartney (2015) When Government Subsidizes Its Own: Collective Bargaining Laws As Agents of Political Mobilization, *American Journal of Political Science* 59(4), 896–911.

Fording, R. C. and D. Patton (2020) The Affordable Care Act and the Diffusion of Policy Feedback: The Case of Medicaid Work Requirements, *RSF: The Russell Sage Foundation Journal of the Social Sciences* 6(2), 131–153.

Freeman, G. P. (1988) Voters, Bureaucrats and the State: On the Autonomy of Social Security Policymaking. In G. D. Nash, N. H. Pugach, and R. F. Tomasson, eds., *Social Security: The First Half-Century* (Albuquerque: University of New Mexico Press), 145–180.

Galvin, D. and J. Hacker (2020) The Political Effects of Policy Drift: Policy Stalemate and American Political Development, *Studies in American Political Development* 34(2), 216–238.

Galvin, D. J. and C. N. Thurston (2017) The Democrats' Misplaced Faith in Policy Feedback. *The Forum*, 15(2), 333–343.

Galvin, D. J. and C. N. Thurston (2018) The Limits of Policy Feedback As a Party-Building Tool. Working Paper No. WP-18–16, Northwestern Institute for Policy Research.

Gangl, M. and A. Ziefle (2015) The Making of a Good Woman: Extended Parental Leave Entitlements and Mothers' Work Commitment in Germany, *American Journal of Sociology* 121(2), 511–563.

Gao, J. (2015) Pernicious Manipulation of Performance Measures in China's Cadre Evaluation System, *China Quarterly* 223, 618–637.

Gao, J. (2016) Bypass the Lying Mouths: How Does the CCP Tackle Information Distortion at Local Levels, *China Quarterly* 228, 950–969.

Gay, C. (2012) Moving to Opportunity: The Political Effects of a Housing Mobility Experiment, *Urban Affairs Review* 48(2), 147–179.

Geddes, B. (1999) What Do We Know About Democratization after Twenty Years? *Annual Review of Political Science* 2, 115–144.

Gidengil, E. (2020) *Take a Number: How Citizens' Encounters with Government Shape Political Engagement* (Montreal and Kingston: McGill-Queen's University Press).

Gilens, M. (1999) *Why Americans Hate Welfare: Race, Media and the Politics of Antipoverty Policy* (Chicago: University of Chicago Press).

Gingrich, J. (2014) Visibility, Values, and Voters: The Informational Role of the Welfare State, *Journal of Politics* 76(2), 565–580.

Gingrich, J. and S. Watson (2016) Privatizing Participation? The Impact of Private Welfare Provision on Democratic Accountability, *Politics and Society* 44(4), 573–613.

Goss, K. A. (2012) *The Paradox of Gender Equality: How American Women's Groups Gained and Lost Their Public Voice* (Ann Arbor: University of Michigan Press).

Green-Pedersen, C. and A. Lindbom (2006) Politics within Paths: Trajectories of Danish and Swedish Earnings-Related Pensions, *Journal of European Social Policy* 16(3), 245–258.

Greif, A. and D. D. Laitin (2004) A Theory of Endogenous Institutional Change, *The American Political Science Review* 98(4), 633–652.

Hacker, J. S. (1998) The Historical Logic of National Health Insurance: Structure and Sequence in the Development of British, Canadian, and U.S. Medical Policy, *Studies in American Political Development* 12(1), 57–130.

Hacker, J. S. (2002) *The Divided Welfare State: The Battle Over Public and Private Social Benefits in the United States* (Cambridge: Cambridge University Press).

Hacker, J. S. (2004) Privatizing Risk without Privatizing the Welfare State: The Hidden Politics of Social Policy Retrenchment in the United States, *The American Political Science Review* 98(2), 243–260.

Hacker, J. S. (2019) *The Great Risk Shift: The New Economic Insecurity and the Decline of the American Dream*, 2nd ed. (Oxford: Oxford University Press).

Hacker, J. S. and P. Pierson (2018) The Dog That Almost Barked: What the ACA Repeal Fight Says About the Resilience of the American Welfare State, *Journal of Health Politics, Policy and Law* 43(4), 551–577.

Hacker, J. S. and P. Pierson (2019) Policy Feedback in an Age of Polarization, *The Annals of the American Academy of Political and Social Science* 685, 8–28.

Hacker, J., P. Pierson, and K. Thelen (2015) Drift and Conversion: Hidden Faces of Institutional Change. In J. Mahoney and K. Thelen, eds., *Advances in Comparative-Historical Analysis* (Cambridge: Cambridge University Press), 180–208.

Hall, P. A. and D. Soskice, eds. (2001) *Varieties of Capitalism: The Institutional Foundations of Comparative Advantage* (Oxford: Oxford University Press).

Hall, P. A. and R. C. R. Taylor (1996) Political Science and the Three New Institutionalisms, *Political Studies* 44(5), 936–957.

Haselswerdt J. (2014) The Lifespan of a Tax Break: Comparing the Durability of Tax Expenditures and Spending Programs, *American Politics Research* 42 (5), 731–759.

Haselswerdt, J. (2017) Expanding Medicaid, Expanding the Electorate: The Affordable Care Act's Short-Term Impact on Political Participation, *Journal of Health Politics, Policy and Law* 42(4), 667–695.

Heclo, H. (1974) *Modern Social Politics in Britain and Sweden: From Relief to Income Maintenance* (New Haven, CT: Yale University Press).

Herd, P. and D. Moynihan (2019) *Administrative Burden* (New York: Russell Sage Foundation).

Hern, E. (2017) *In the Gap the State Left: Policy Feedback, Collective Behavior and Political Participation in Zambia.* Studies in Comparative International Development. New York: Russell Sage Foundation.

Hertel-Fernandez, A. (2019) *State Capture: How Conservative Activists, Big Businesses, and Wealthy Donors Reshaped the American States – and the Nation* (Oxford: Oxford University Press).

Herweg, N., N. Zahariadis, and R. Zohlnhöfer (2018) The Multiple Streams Framework: Foundations, Refinements and Empirical Applications. In C. M. Weible and P. A. Sabatier, eds., *Theories of the Policy Process*, 4th ed. (New York and London: Routledge), 17–54.

Hjortskov, M., S. C. Andersen, and M. Jakobsen (2018) Citizens through Coproduction: Evidence from a Randomized Field Trial, *American Journal of Political Science* 62(3), 597–609.

Hobbs, W. R. and D. J. Hopkins (2021) Offsetting Policy Feedback Effects: Evidence from the Affordable Care Act, *The Journal of Politics*, 83(4), 1800–1817.

Hopkins, D. J. and K. Parish (2019) The Medicaid Expansion and Attitudes toward the Affordable Care Act, *Public Opinion Quarterly*, 83(1), 123–134.

Howard, C. (1997) *The Hidden Welfare State: Tax Expenditures and Social Policy in the United States* (Princeton, NJ: Princeton University Press).

Howard, C. (2007) *The Welfare State Nobody Knows: Debunking Myths about U.S. Social Policy* (Princeton, NJ: Princeton University Press).

Howlett, M. (2014) From the "Old" to the "New" Policy Design: Design Thinking beyond Markets and Collaborative Governance, *Policy Sciences*, 29, 187–207.

Howlett, M., G. Capano, and M. Ramesh (2018) Designing for Robustness: Surprise, Agility and Improvisation in Policy Design, *Policy and Society* 37 (4), 405–421.

Howlett, M., A. McConnell, and A. Perl (2015) Streams and Stages: Reconciling Kingdom and Policy Process Theory, *European Journal of Political Research* 54(3), 419–434.

Howlett, M. and I. Mukherjee, eds. (2017) *Handbook of Policy Formulation* (Cheltenham: Edward Elgar).

Im, D. and T. Meng (2016) The Policy-Opinion Nexus: The Impact of Social Protection Programs on Welfare Policy Preferences in China, *International Journal of Public Opinion Research* 28(2), 241–268.

Immergut, E. M. (1992) *Health Politics: Interests and Institutions in Western Europe* (New York: Cambridge University Press).

Immergut, E. M. (1998) The Theoretical Core of the New Institutionalism, *Politics and Society* 26(1), 5–34.

Immergut, E. M., K. M. Anderson, and I. Schulze, eds. (2007) *The Handbook of West European Pension Politics* (Oxford: Oxford University Press).

Jacobs, A. M. (2011) *Governing for the Long Term: Democracy and the Politics of Investment* (New York: Cambridge University Press).

Jacobs, A. M. (2016) Social Policy Dynamics. In O. Fioretos, T. G. Falleti, and A. Sheingate, eds., *The Oxford Handbook of Historical Institutionalism* (Oxford: Oxford University Press), 142–162.

Jacobs, A. M. and R. K. Weaver (2015) When Policies Undo Themselves: Self-Undermining Feedback As a Source of Policy Change, *Governance* 28(4), 441–457.

Jacobs, L. R. and S. Mettler (2018) When and How New Policy Creates New Politics: Examining the Feedback Effects of the Affordable Care Act on Public Opinion, *Perspectives on Politics* 16(2), 345–363.

Jenkins-Smith, H. C., D. Nohrstedt, C. M. Weible, and K. Ingold (2018) The Advocacy Coalition Framework: An Overview of the Research Program. In C. M. Weible and P. A. Sabatier, eds., *Theories of the Policy Process*, 4th ed. (New York and London: Routledge), 135–172.

Jones, B. D. and F. R. Baumgartner (2005) *The Politics of Attention: How Government Prioritizes Problems* (Chicago: University of Chicago Press).

Jones, B. D. and Baumgartner, F. R. (2012) From There to Here: Punctuated Equilibrium to the General Punctuation Thesis to a Theory of Government Information Processing, *Policy Studies Journal* 40(1), 1–20.

Jones, B. D., F. R. Baumgartner, C. Breunig et al. (2009), A General Empirical Law of Public Budgets: A Comparative Analysis, *American Journal of Political Science* 53(4), 855–873.

Jordan, A. and E. Matt (2014) Designing Policies That Intentionally Stick: Policy Feedback in a Changing Climate, *Policy Sciences* 47(3), 227–247.

Kahneman, D. and A. Tversky (1979) Prospect Theory: An Analysis of Decision under Risk, *Econometrica* 47(2), 263–291.

Karapin, R. (2014) Wind-Power Development in Germany and the United States: Structural Factors, Multiple-Stream Convergence, and Turning Points. In A. Duit, ed., *State and Environment: The Comparative Study of Environmental Governance* (Cambridge, MA: MIT Press), 111–137.

Karch, A. and S. Rose (2017) States As Stakeholders: Federalism, Policy Feedback, and Government Elites, *Studies in American Political Development* 31(1), 47–67.

Karch, A. and S. Rose (2019) *Responsive States: Federalism and American Public Policy* (Cambridge: Cambridge University Press).

Kay, S. J. (1999) Unexpected Privatizations: Politics and Social Security Reform in the Southern Cone, *Comparative Politics* 31(4), 403–422.

Kellow, A. (2018) From Policy Typologies to Policy Feedback. In H. K. Colebatch and R. Hoppe, eds., *Handbook on Policy, Process and Governing* (Cheltenham: Edward Elgar), 457–472.

Kingdon, J. W. (1984) *Agendas, Alternatives, and Public Policies* (New York: HarperCollins).

Kitschelt, H. (1986) Political Opportunity Structures and Political Protest: Anti-nuclear Movements in Four Democracies, *British Journal of Political Science* 16(1), 57–85.

Klein, J. (2003) *For All These Rights: Business, Labor, and the Shaping of America's Public-Private Welfare State* (Princeton, NJ: Princeton University Press).

Kreitzer, R. J., A. J. Hamilton, and C. J. Tolbert (2014) Does Policy Adoption Change Opinions on Minority Rights? The Effects of Legalizing Same-Sex Marriage, *Political Research Quarterly* 67(4), 795–808.

Kumlin, S. (2004) *The Personal and the Political: How Personal Welfare State Experiences Affect Political Trust and Ideology* (New York: Palgrave Macmillan).

Lam, W. F. and Chan, K. N. (2015) How Authoritarianism Intensifies Punctuated Equilibrium: The Dynamics of Policy Attention in Hong Kong, *Governance*, 28(4), 549–570.

Larsen, E. G. (2018) Welfare Retrenchment and Government Support: Evidence from a Natural Experiment, *European Sociological Review* 34(1), 40–51.

Larsen, E. G. (2019) Policy Feedback Effects on Mass Publics: A Quantitative Review, *Policy Studies Journal* 47(2), 372–394.

Larsen, E. G. (2020) Personal Politics? Healthcare Policies, Personal Experiences and Government Attitudes, *Journal of European Social Policy* 30(4), 467–479.

Lecours. A., ed. (2005) *New Institutionalism: Theory and Analysis* (Toronto: University of Toronto Press).

Lee, F. E. (2009) *Beyond Ideology: Politics, Principles, and Partisanship in the US Senate* (Chicago: University of Chicago Press).

Lerman, A. E. and K. T. McCabe (2017) Personal Experience and Public Opinion: A Theory and Test of Conditional Policy Feedback, *Journal of Politics* 79(2), 624–641.

Lerman, A. E., M. L. Sadin, and S. Trachtman. (2017) Policy Uptake As Political Behavior: Evidence from the Affordable Care Act, *American Political Science Review* 111(4), 755–770.

Leutert, W. (2021) Innovation through Iteration: Policy Feedback Loops in China's Economic Reform, *World Development*, 138, 1–11.

Levitsky, S. and L. Way (2010) *Competitive Authoritarianism: Hybrid Regimes after the Cold War* (Cambridge: Cambridge University Press).

Li, Z. and X. Wu (2018) Social Policy and Political Trust: Evidence from the New Rural Pension Scheme in China, *China Quarterly* 235, 644–668.

Lieberman, R. C. (1995) Social Construction (Continued), *American Political Science Review* 89(2), 437–441.

Lindh, A. (2015) Public Opinion against Markets? Attitudes towards Market Distribution of Social Services: A Comparison of 17 Countries, *Social Policy and Administration* 49(7), 887–910.

Lockwood, M. (2013) The Political Sustainability of Climate Policy: The Case of the UK Climate Change Act, *Global Environmental Change* 23(5), 1339–1348.

Lowi, T. J. (1964) American Business, Public Policy, Case-Studies, and Political Theory, *World Politics* 16(4), 677–715.

Lowi, T. J. (1972) Four Systems of Policy, Politics, and Choice, *Public Administration Review* 32(4), 298–310.

Lowi, T. J. (2009) *Arenas of Power* (Boulder, CO: Paradigm Publishers).

Lu, X. (2014) Social Policy and Regime Legitimacy: The Effects of Education Reform in China, *American Political Science Review* 108(2), 423–437.

Lynch, J. (2006) *Age in the Welfare State: The Origins of Social Spending on Pensioners, Workers, and Children* (New York: Cambridge University Press).

Lynch, L. R. (2011) *One Nation under AARP: The Fight over Medicare, Social Security, and America's Future* (Berkeley: University of California Press).

MacLean, L. M. (2011) State Retrenchment and the Exercise of Citizenship in Africa, *Comparative Political Studies* 44(9), 1238–1266.

Maltby, E. (2017) The Political Origins of Racial Inequality, *Political Research Quarterly* 70(3), 535–548.

Maltzman, F. and C. E. Shipan (2012) Beyond Legislative Productivity: Enactment Conditions, Subsequent Conditions, and the Shape and Life of the Law. In J. A. Jenkins and E. M. Patashnik, eds., *Living Legislation: Durability, Change, and the Politics of American Lawmaking* (Chicago: University of Chicago Press), 111–134.

Manacorda, M., E. Miguel, and A. Vigorito (2011) Government Transfers and Political Support, *American Economic Journal: Applied Economics* 3(3), 1–28.

Marshall, T. H. (1964) *Class, Citizenship, and Social Development* (Chicago: University of Chicago Press).

Mau, S. (2003) *The Moral Economy of Welfare States: Britain and Germany Compared* (London: Routledge).

Mau, S. (2004) Welfare Regimes and the Norms of Exchange, *Current Sociology* 52(1), 53–74.

McCabe, K. T. (2016) Attitude Responsiveness and Partisan Bias: Direct Experience with the Affordable Care Act, *Political Behavior* 38(4), 861–882.

McDonagh, E. (2010) It Takes a State: A Policy Feedback Model of Women's Political Representation, *Perspectives on Politics* 8(1), 69–91.

Mettler, S. (2005) *Soldiers to Citizens: The G.I. Bill and the Making of the Greatest Generation* (New York: Oxford University Press).

Mettler, S. (2011) *The Submerged State: How Invisible Government Policies Undermine American Democracy* (Chicago: University of Chicago Press).

Mettler, S. (2018) *The Government-Citizen Disconnect* (New York: Russell Sage Foundation).

Mettler S. (2019) Making What Government Does Apparent to Citizens: Policy Feedback Effects, Their Limitations, and How They Might Be Facilitated, *The Annals of the American Academy of Political and Social Science* 685, 30–46.

Mettler, S. and M. SoRelle (2014) Policy Feedback Theory. In P. A. Sabatier and C. M. Weible, eds., *Theories of the Policy Process*, 3rd ed. (Boulder, CO: Westview Press), 151–181.

Mettler, S. and M. SoRelle (2018) Policy Feedback Theory. In P. A. Sabatier and C. M. Weible, eds., *Theories of the Policy Process*, 4th ed. (New York: Westview Press), 103–134.

Mettler, S. and J. Soss (2004) The Consequences of Public Policy for Democratic Citizenship: Bridging Policy Studies and Mass Politics, *Perspectives on Politics* 2(1), 55–73.

Michener, J. (2018) *Fragmented Democracy: Medicaid, Federalism, and Unequal Politics* (New York: Cambridge University Press).

Michener, J. (2019) Policy Feedback in a Racialized Policy, *Policy Studies Journal* 47(2), 423–450.

Mons, U., G. E. Nagelhout, R. Guignard et al. (2012) Comprehensive Smoke-Free Policies Attract More Support from Smokers in Europe than Partial Policies, *European Journal of Public Health* 22(suppl. 1), 10–16.

Moore, B. and A. Jordan (2020) Disaggregating the Dependent Variable in Policy Feedback Research: An Analysis of the EU Emissions Trading System, *Policy Sciences* 53(2), 291–307.

Morgan, K. J. and A. L. Campbell (2011) *The Delegated Welfare State: Medicare, Markets, and the Governance of American Social Policy* (New York: Oxford University Press).

Moynihan, D. P. and J. Soss (2014) Policy Feedback and the Politics of Administration, *Public Administration Review* 74(3), 320–332.

Myles, J. and P. Pierson. (2001) The Comparative Political Economy of Pension Reform. In P. Pierson, ed., *The New Politics of the Welfare State* (Oxford: Oxford University Press), 305–333.

North, D. C. (1990) *Institutions, Institutional Change and Economic Performance* (Cambridge: Cambridge University Press).

Oberlander, J. (2003) *The Political Life of Medicare* (Chicago: University of Chicago Press).

Oberlander, J. and R. K. Weaver (2015) Unraveling from Within? The Affordable Care Act and Self-Undermining Policy Feedbacks, *The Forum* 13(1), 37–62.

Ojeda, C. (2015) Depression and Political Participation, *Social Science Quarterly* 96(5), 1226–1243.

Olorunnipa, T. and L. Rein (2020) Trump Denied He Wanted His Name on Stimulus Checks: Here's How It Happened, *Washington Post*, April 16.

Orloff, A. S. (1993) *The Politics of Pensions: A Comparative Analysis of Britain, Canada, and the United States, 1880–1940* (Madison: University of Wisconsin Press).

Orren, K. and S. Skowronek (2004) *The Search for American Political Development* (New York: Cambridge University Press).

Pacheco, J. (2013) Attitudinal Policy Feedback and Public Opinion: The Impact of Smoking Ban on Attitudes towards Smokers, Secondhand Smoke, and Antismoking Policies, *Public Opinion Quarterly* 77(3), 714–734.

Pacheco, J. and J. Fletcher (2015) Incorporating Health into Studies of Political Behavior: Evidence for Turnout and Partisanship, *Political Research Quarterly* 68(1), 104–116.

Pantoja, A. D., R. Ramirez, and G. M. Segura (2001) Citizens by Choice, Voters by Necessity: Patterns in Political Mobilization by Naturalized Latinos, *Political Research Quarterly* 54(4), 729–750.

Patashnik, E. M. (1997) Unfolding Promises: Trust Funds and the Politics of Precommitment, *Political Science Quarterly*, 112(3), 431–452.

Patashnik, E. M. (2008) *Reforms at Risk: What Happens After Major Policy Changes Are Enacted* (Princeton, NJ: Princeton University Press).

Patashnik, E. M. (2019) Limiting Policy Backlash: Strategies for Taming Countercoalitions in an Era of Polarization, *The Annals of the American Academy of Political and Social Science* 685, 47–63.

Patashnik, E. M. and R. K. Weaver (2021) Policy Analysis and Political Sustainability, *Policy Studies Journal* 49(4), 1110–1134.

Patashnik, E. and J. Zelizer (2013) The Struggle to Remake Politics: Liberal Reform and the Limits of Policy Feedback in the Contemporary American State, *Perspectives on Politics* 11(4), 1071–1087.

Perera, I. (2020) The French Welfare State Revisited: The Puzzling Politics of Mental Health Policy, *French Politics* 18(4), 405–415.

Perera, I. (2021a) Interest Group Governance and Policy Agendas, *Governance*. https://doi.org/10.1111/gove.12615.

Perera, I. (2021b) What Doctors Want: A Comment on the Financial Preferences of Organized Medicine, *Journal of Health Policy, Politics, and Law* 46(4), 731–745.

Perl, A. and M. I. Burke (2018) Does Institutional Entrenchment Shape Instrument Adjustment? Assessing Instrument Constituency Influences on American and Australian Motor Fuel Taxation, *Policy and Society* 37(1), 90–107.

Peters, B. G. (2011) *Institutional Theory in Political Science: The New Institutionalism*, 3rd ed. (London: Continuum).

Petrocik, J. R. (1996) Issue Ownership in Presidential Elections, with a 1980 Case Study, *American Journal of Political Science* 40(3), 825–850.

Pierson, P. (1993) When Effect Becomes Cause: Policy Feedback and Political Change, *World Politics* 45(4), 595–628.

Pierson, P. (1994) *Dismantling the Welfare State? Reagan, Thatcher, and the Politics of Retrenchment* (New York: Cambridge University Press).

Pierson, P. (2000a) Increasing Returns, Path Dependence, and the Study of Politics, *The American Political Science Review* 94(2), 251–267.

Pierson, P. (2000b) The Limits of Design: Explaining Institutional Origins and Change, *Governance* 13(4), 475–499.

Pierson, P. (2004a) Ahead of Its Time: On Martha Derthick's Policymaking for Social Security, *PS: Political Science and Politics* 37(3), 441–442.

Pierson, P. (2004b) *Politics in Time: History, Institutions, and Social Analysis* (Princeton, NJ: Princeton University Press).

Pierson, P. and R. K. Weaver (1993) Imposing Losses in Pension Policy. In R. Kent and B. A. Rockman Weaver, eds., *Do Institutions Matter?*

Government Capabilities in the United States and Abroad (Washington, DC: Brookings Institution), 110–150.

Pop-Eleches, C. and G. Pop-Eleches (2012) Targeted Government Spending and Political Preferences, *Quarterly Journal of Political Science* 7(3), 285–320.

Princen, S. (2013) Punctuated Equilibrium Theory and the European Union, *Journal of European Public Policy* 20(6), 854–870.

Rabe, B. G. and R. L. Hampton (2016) Trusting in the Future: The Re-emergence of State Trust Funds in the Shale Era, *Energy Research and Social Science* 20, 117–127.

Rein, L. (2020) Coming to Your $1,200 Relief Check: Donald J. Trump's Name, *Washington Post*, April 15.

Rendleman, H. E. and J. Yoder (2021) Do Government Benefits Affect Officeholders' Electoral Fortunes? Evidence from State Earned Income Tax Credits. Working Paper, Harvard University, March 24.

Ricks, J. I. and T. Laiprakobsup (2021) Becoming Citizens: Policy Feedback and the Transformation of the Thai Rice Farmer, *Journal of Rural Studies* 81, 139–147.

Rodan, G. (2018) *Participation without Democracy: Containing Conflict in Southeast Asia* (Ithaca, NY: Cornell University Press).

Rose, S. (2013) *Financing Medicaid: Federalism and the Growth of America's Health Care Safety Net* (Ann Arbor: University of Michigan Press).

Rosenbloom, D., J. Meadowcroft, and B. Cashore (2019) Stability and Climate Policy? Harnessing Insights on Path Dependence, Policy Feedback, and Transition Pathways, *Energy Research and Social Science* 50, 168–178.

Rosenthal, A. (2019) Conflicting Messages: Multiple Policy Experiences and Political Participation, *Policy Studies Journal*, October 3.

Rosenthal, A. (2021) Submerged for Some? Government Visibility, Race, and American Political Trust, *Perspectives on Politics* 19(4), 1098–1114.

Sances, M. W. and J. D. Clinton (2021) Policy Effects, Partisanship, and Elections: How Medicaid Expansion Affected Opinions of the Affordable Care Act, *Journal of Politics* 83(2), 498–514.

Schattschneider, E. E. (1935) *Politics, Pressures and the Tariff* (New York: Prentice Hall).

Schneider, A. L. and H. M. Ingram (1993) Social Construction of Target Populations, *American Political Science Review* 87(2), 333–347.

Schneider, A. L. and H. M. Ingram (2005) Public Policy and the Social Construction of Deservedness. In A. L. Schneider and H. M. Ingram, eds., *Deserving and Entitled: Social Constructions and Public Policy* (Albany: State University of New York Press), 1–28.

Schneider, A. L. and H. M. Ingram (2019) Social Constructions, Anticipatory Feedback Strategies, and Deceptive Public Policy, *Policy Studies Journal* 47 (2), 206–236.

Seeberg, H. B. (2017) How Stable Is Political Parties' Issue Ownership? A Cross-Time, Cross-National Analysis, *Political Studies* 65(2), 475–492.

Sewerin, S., D. Béland, and B. Cashore (2020) Designing Policy for the Long Term: Agency, Policy Feedback and Policy Change, *Policy Sciences* 53(2), 243–252.

Shore, J. (2019) *The Welfare State and the Democratic Citizen: How Social Policies Shape Political Equality* (London: Palgrave Macmillan).

Shore, J. (2020) Singled Out or Drawn In? Social Policies and Lone Mothers' Political Engagement, *Politics and Gender* 16(2), 471–497.

Simonovits, G., N. Malhotra, R. Ye Lee, and A. Healy (2021) The Effect of Distributive Politics on Electoral Participation: Evidence from 70 Million Agricultural Payments, *Political Behavior* 43(2), 737–750.

Sinha. A. (2019) A Theory of Reform Consolidation in India: From Crisis-Induced Reforms to Strategic Internationalization, *India Review* 18(1), 54–87.

Skocpol, T. (1990) Sustainable Social Policy: Fighting Poverty without Poverty Programs, *The American Prospect* 1(2), 58–70.

Skocpol. T. (1992) *Protecting Soldiers and Mothers: The Political Origins of Social Policy in the United States* (Cambridge, MA: The Belknap Press of the Harvard University Press).

Skogstad, G. (2017) Policy Feedback and Self-Reinforcing and Self-Undermining Processes in EU Biofuels Policy, *Journal of European Public Policy* 24(1), 21–41.

Skogstad, G. (2020) Mixed Feedback Dynamics and the USA Renewable Fuel Standard: The Roles of Policy Design and Administrative Agency, *Policy Sciences* 53(2), 349–369.

Skowronek, S. (1982) *Building a New American State: The Expansion of National Administrative Capacities, 1877–1920* (Cambridge: Cambridge University Press).

Soroka, S. N. and C. Wlezien (2004) Opinion Representation and Policy Feedback: Canada in Comparative Perspective, *Canadian Journal of Political Science* 37(3), 531–559.

Soroka, S. N. and C. Wlezien (2010) *Degrees of Democracy* (New York: Cambridge University Press).

Soss, J. (1999) Lessons of Welfare: Policy Design, Political Learning, and Political Action, *American Political Science Review* 93(2), 363–380.

Soss, J. and S. F. Schram (2007) A Public Transformed? Welfare Reform As Policy Feedback, *American Political Science Review* 101(1), 111–127.

Steensland, B. (2008) *The Failed Welfare Revolution: America's Struggle Over Guaranteed Income Policy* (Princeton, NJ: Princeton University Press).

Steinmo, S. (1996) *Taxation and Democracy: Swedish, British and American Approaches to Financing the Modern State* (New Haven, CT: Yale University Press).

Steinmo, S., K. Thelen, and F. Longstreth, eds. (1992) *Structuring Politics: Historical Institutionalism in Comparative Analysis* (Cambridge: Cambridge University Press).

Stimson, J. A. (2004) *Tides of Consent* (New York: Cambridge University Press).

Stokes, L. C. (2020) *Short-Circuiting Policy: Interest Groups and the Battle Over Clean Energy and Climate Policy in the American States* (Oxford: Oxford University Press).

Suzuki, K. (2020) Government Retrenchment and Citizen Participation in Volunteering: A Cross-National Analysis of OECD Countries, *Public Policy and Administration* 35(3), 266–288.

Svallfors, S. (1997) Worlds of Welfare and Attitudes to Redistribution: A Comparison of Eight Western Countries, *European Sociological Review* 13(3), 283–304.

Svallfors, S. (2006) *The Moral Economy of Class: Class and Attitudes in Comparative Perspective* (Stanford, CA: Stanford University Press).

Svallfors, S. (2007) *The Political Sociology of the Welfare State: Institutions, Social Cleavages, and Orientations* (Stanford, CA: Stanford University Press).

Svallfors, S. (2010) Policy Feedback, Generational Replacement, and Attitudes to State Intervention: Eastern and Western Germany, 1990–2006, *European Political Science Review* 2(1), 119–135.

Sykes, J., K. Kriz, K. Edin, and S. Halpern-Meekin (2015) Dignity and Dreams: What the Earned Income Tax Credit (EITC) Means to Low-Income Families, *American Sociological Review* 80(2), 243–267.

Thelen, K. (2003) How Institutionalism Evolves: Insights from Comparative Historical Analysis. In J. Mahoney and J. Rueschemeyer, eds., *Comparative Historical Analysis in the Social Sciences* (New York: Cambridge University Press), 208–240.

Thelen, K. (2004) *How Institutions Evolve: The Political Economy of Skills in Germany, Britain, the United States, and Japan* (Cambridge: Cambridge University Press).

Thurston, C. N. (2015) Policy Feedback in the Public-Private Welfare State: Advocacy Groups and Access to Government Homeownership Programs, 1934–1954, *Studies in American Political Development* 29(2), 250–267.

Thurston, C. N. (2018) Black Lives Matter, American Political Development, and the Politics of Visibility, *Politics, Groups, and Identities* 6(1), 162–170.

Tsebelis, G. (2002) *Veto Players: How Political Institutions Work* (Princeton, NJ: Princeton University Press).

Tynes, S. R. (1996) *Turning Points in Social Security: From "Cruel Hoax" to "Sacred Entitlement"* (Palo Alto, CA: Stanford University Press).

Valelly, R. M., S. Mettler, and R. C. Lieberman, eds. (2016) *The Oxford Handbook of American Political Development* (New York: Oxford University Press).

Vannutelli, S. (2019) Fighting Inequality or Buying Votes? The Political Economy of Redistributive Transfers: Evidence from the Italian Earned Income Tax Credit. Working Paper, Boston University, January 31.

Verba, S., K. L. Schlozman, and H. Brady. (1995) *Voice and Equality: Civil Voluntarism in American Politics* (Cambridge, MA: Harvard University Press).

Wallace, J. (2013) Cities, Redistribution, and Authoritarian Regime Survival, *The Journal of Politics* 75(3), 632–645.

Wallace, J. (2016) Juking the Stats? Authoritarian Information Problems in China, *British Journal of Political Science* 46(1), 11–29.

Watson, S. (2015) Does Welfare Conditionality Reduce Democratic Participation, *Comparative Political Studies* 48(5), 645–686.

Weaver, C. L. (1982) *The Crisis in Social Security: Economic and Political Origins* (Durham, NC: Duke University Press).

Weaver, R. K. (1988) *Automatic Government: The Politics of Indexation* (Washington, DC: The Brookings Institution).

Weaver, R. K. (2000) *Ending Welfare As We Know It* (Washington, DC: Brookings Institution).

Weaver, R. K. (2010) Paths and Forks or Chutes and Ladders? Negative Feedbacks and Policy Regime Change, *Journal of Public Policy* 30(2), 136–162.

Weaver, R. K. (2015) Policy Feedbacks and Pension Policy Change. In C. Torp, ed., *Challenges of Aging: Retirement, Pensions and Intergenerational Justice* (Basingstoke: Palgrave Macmillan).

Weaver, R. K. (2016) Privileging Policy Change? Sustaining Automatic Stabilizing Mechanisms in Public Pensions, *Social Policy and Administration* 50(2), 148–164.

Weaver, R. K. (2018) The Nays Have It: How Rampant Blame Generating Distorts American Policy and Politics, *Political Science Quarterly* 133(2), 259–289.

Weaver, R. K. (2020) Policy Dynamics Under Federalism: A Framework for Analysis, *Publius: A Journal of Federalism* 50(2), 157–187.

Weaver, R. K. and B. Rockman, eds. (1993) *Do Institutions Matter? Government Capabilities in the U.S. and Abroad* (Washington, DC: Brookings Institution).

Weaver, V. and A. Lerman (2010) Political Consequences of the Carceral State, *American Political Science Review* 104(4), 817–833.

Weaver, V. M. (2007) Frontlash: Race and the Development of Punitive Crime Policy, *Studies in American Political Development* 21(2), 230–265.

Weaver, V. M. and A. Geller (2019) De-policing America's Youth: Disrupting Criminal Justice Policy Feedbacks That Distort Power and Derail Prospects. *The Annals of the American Academy of Political and Social Science* 685, 190–226.

Weir, M. (1992) *Politics and Jobs: The Boundaries of Employment Policy in the United States* (Princeton, NJ: Princeton University Press).

Weir, M., A.S. Orloff, and T. Skocpol, eds. (1988) *The Politics of Social Policy in the United States* (Princeton, NJ: Princeton University Press).

White, A. (2016) When Threat Mobilizes: Immigration Enforcement and Latino Voter Turnout, *Political Behavior* 38(2), 355–382.

Wilson, J. Q. (1973) *Political Organizations* (New York: Basic Books).

Wilson, J. Q. (1991) *Bureaucracy: What Government Agencies Do and Why They Do It* (New York: Basic Books).

Winter, N. J. G. (2006) Beyond Welfare: Framing and the Racialization of White Opinion on Social Security, *American Journal of Political Science* 50(2), 400–420.

Wlezien, C. (1995) The Public As Thermostat: Dynamics of Preferences for Spending, *American Journal of Political Science* 39(4), 981–1000.

Zhu, L. and C. S. Lipsmeyer (2015) Policy Feedback and Economic Risk: The Influence of Privatization on Social Policy Preferences, *Journal of European Public Policy* 22(10), 1489–1511.

Acknowledgments

The editors thank Mathieu Lavault for the copy-editing assistance and the anonymous reviewers for their comments and suggestions.

Public Policy

M. Ramesh
National University of Singapore (NUS)

M. Ramesh is UNESCO Chair on Social Policy Design at the Lee Kuan Yew School of Public Policy, NUS. His research focuses on governance and social policy in East and Southeast Asia, in addition to public policy institutions and processes. He has published extensively in reputed international journals. He is Co-editor of Policy and Society and Policy Design and Practice.

Michael Howlett
Simon Fraser University, British Columbia

Michael Howlett is Burnaby Mountain Professor and Canada Research Chair (Tier 1) in the Department of Political Science, Simon Fraser University. He specialises in public policy analysis, and resource and environmental policy. He is currently editor-in-chief of Policy Sciences and co-editor of the Journal of Comparative Policy Analysis, Policy and Society and Policy Design and Practice.

Xun WU
Hong Kong University of Science and Technology

Xun WU is Professor and Head of the Division of Public Policy at the Hong Kong University of Science and Technology. He is a policy scientist whose research interests include policy innovations, water resource management and health policy reform. He has been involved extensively in consultancy and executive education, his work involving consultations for the World Bank and UNEP.

Judith Clifton
University of Cantabria

Judith Clifton is Professor of Economics at the University of Cantabria, Spain. She has published in leading policy journals and is editor-in-chief of the Journal of Economic Policy Reform. Most recently, her research enquires how emerging technologies can transform public administration, a forward-looking cutting-edge project which received €3.5 million funding from the Horizon2020 programme.

Eduardo Araral
National University of Singapore (NUS)

Eduardo Araral is widely published in various journals and books and has presented in forty conferences. He is currently Co-Director of the Institute of Water Policy at the Lee Kuan Yew School of Public Policy, NUS, and is a member of the editorial board of Journal of Public Administration Research and Theory and the board of the Public Management Research Association.

About the Series

Elements in Public Policy is a concise and authoritative collection of assessments of the state of the art and future research directions in public policy research, as well as substantive new research on key topics. Edited by leading scholars in the field, the series is an ideal medium for reflecting on and advancing the understanding of critical issues in the public sphere. Collectively, it provides a forum for broad and diverse coverage of all major topics in the field while integrating different disciplinary and methodological approaches.

Cambridge Elements ☰

Public Policy

Elements in the Series

A full series listing is available at: www.cambridge.org/EPPO

Printed in the United States
by Baker & Taylor Publisher Services